When The Spirit

When The Spirit Takes Over

By

B R Taylor

2021

First Printing, 2021

Cover design
by
B R Taylor

ISBN : 9798735639329

Preface

I have always had a deep fascination concerning the big questions of life. Why are we here? Who made us? And, where do we go after we die? Questions which modern society seems eager to brush aside in favour of a continual stream of entertainment through celebrity gossip, political infighting and ball games. I was aware, long ago, that my inquisitive mind and nature were part of a very small minority. To satisfy my thirst for answers, I ultimately found myself on the fringes of society, living a rather unconventional life far away from my original home.

Contents

Introduction 1

Chapter 1. When the spirit takes over 2

    Difference between spirit and soul 2

    Terminal Lucidity 4

    Case 1. Anna Katherina Ehmer 4

    Case 2. 1822, 6 year old boy 6

    Case 3. Old Alzheimer's patient 6

    The death of my own father 10

    Case 4. Voice telling me to move 12

    Cases 5,6 & 7. A helping hand 13

    Cases 8,9 & 10. I saw them standing there 15

    Cases 11 & 12. I left my body 17

    Soul mates 20

    Mid-life crisis 25

    Notes for chapter 1 27

Chapter 2. Animals & pets 29

    Dog's senses 33

    Saint John Bosco 40

Notes for chapter 2 46

Chapter 3. Reincarnation 48

Dalai Lama 53

Past life memories 55

The case of James Leininger 56

The case of Titu Singh 61

Past life regression 63

Genius children 70

Famous prodigies 71

Wolfgang Amadeus Mozart 71

Notes for chapter 3 86

Chapter 4. Meditation 88

Reprogramming the subconscious 92

The power of collective meditation 98

Moon cycles and phases 107

The full Moon 110

Altered consciousness through meditation 113

Notes for chapter 4 116

Chapter 5. Spirit possession 117

Haitian Vodou 118

Jinn & spirits in Islam 122

Jinn possession 128

Spirit possession within Catholicism 130

Exorcism 136

The case of Emma Schmidt 1928 139

Spirit possession in Buddhism 147

Tibetan oracles 155

Incense 158

Notes for chapter 5 161

Chapter 6. Karma 162

Examples of Karma 171

Importance of forgiveness 173

Notes for chapter 6 175

Chapter 7. Near-death experiences 176

The case of Pam Reynolds 177

The case of Barbara Bartolome 179

The case of Howard Storm 181

The case of Jane Thompson 187

Notes for chapter 7 191

Chapter 8. Psychoactive drugs 192

    Accounts of Ayahuasca and hallucinogenic drugs .. 195

    Albert Hofmann & LSD 198

    Notes for chapter 8 202

Conclusion 203

Author's Bio 211

Other books by this author 212

Websites by this author 215

When The Spirit Takes Over

Introduction

The idea for this book came about from my observations in relation to my own father's death. At the beginning of 2008 my father came down with a severe case of, what appeared to be, the flu. For weeks his energy levels were so depleted, all he could do was to lay in bed. This took a toll on both his appearance and his usual demeanour. As my father slowly recovered his character appeared to display signs of being connected to other forms of conscious influence. In the meantime his doctor had performed numerous test on him to determine what was causing his lingering illness and lack of energy. When the tests came back all they found was a mild form of prostrate cancer which would be a simple procedure to rectify. He was booked in for the operation later in the year. However, during the months leading up to the operation he began to put all his affairs in order, numerous folders appeared for organising and arranging various areas of paperwork with instructions and contingency plans for my mother and the family if he should suddenly die. At this point he was only 66 years old, a non smoker and he very rarely drank. Most of his life he had paid attention to his diet with regular bouts of exercise, usually in the form of jogging. His family, as onlookers, regarded all this organised preparation as unnecessary. It was as though a deeper side of his subconscious had taken over the reins of his faculties in order to tie up many loose ends and prepare those around him for what was to come. A few months before he was scheduled to have his prostrate operated on he collapsed from a heart attack, in the living room of his home, while alone. My mother who was usually with him had only gone out to attend a two hour weekly art class, and on her return he was already dead.

The objective of this book is to analyse and investigate that aspect of our consciousness which appears to work outside our familiar earthly constraints of time and space; A connection to a realm which appears to have some form of awareness to the past, the present and the future.

Chapter 1. When the spirit takes over.

As a person's life draws to a close there may be certain tasks which, although seem unimportant to most of the living, could, for a variety of reasons, be a necessary part of the dying process, to help the individual move over to the next realm without hindrance. The transition between soul and spirit consciousness, for most people, is an undiluted crossover, where the person's awareness moves from the body soul into the spirit, breaking the connection as they leave the soul body behind. However, for some, the conscious crossover is not altogether black and white, it contains moments of integration, where the soul body takes on some of the paranormal characteristics of the spirit, as though the spirit is purposely interfacing with the physical realm in order to initiate and perform certain tasks. Some of these interactions, although rare, have been witnessed and documented by the dying person's close friends and family. In some cases, where a person had died unexpectedly, friends and family members have reported strange and unusual behaviour by the deceased, days or even months prior to their unexpected death. Many people working with the dying, in care homes and hospitals have witnessed what is referred to as terminal lucidity, a condition where a person experiences increased mental clarity and alertness during the dying process, lasting minutes, hours or even days, prior to their death. This could very well be a point in someone's life when the spirit takes over. Throughout our lives most of us will experience some degree of interaction with our spiritual consciousness, whether it be the occasional gut feeling, guidance from our own spirit, help from a guardian spirit or even heightened awareness during times of terminal lucidity when the veil between this world and the next narrows.

Difference between the spirit and the soul

There are many different opinions and interpretations as to what the soul and spirit are, with many people confusing the two terms, often interchanging one with the other. To keep it simple and easy to understand, the difference can be viewed as two aspects of our consciousness. The soul being our physical, Earth bound, conscious tether to universal consciousness or Logos, while the spirit is our eternal consciousness, which exists outside the physical constraints of time and space, experiencing the past, the present and the future simultaneously. The soul has for millennia been associated with the Sun or Sol, which energises and gives life to our soul perspective or focal awareness. When the Sun appears on the horizon, most of us awake from our slumber back into focal awareness, to rise from our beds and to stand on the Earth with the soles of our feet. This soul aspect of consciousness is constrained by lineal time and the physical restrictions of the space we inhabit. The spirit, on the other hand, exists beyond the physical, and as such is part of a collective consciousness which has greater scope outside earthly constraints. This is our tether to the spirit realm, and through the subconscious we have the potential and ability to connect with it. In the ancient world of Gnosticism, many believed in a creator God, of the spiritual realm, and a material God, or craftsman, fashioning the physical realm.

"According to the Gnostics, the Demiurge was able to endow man only with psyche, sensuous soul; only the True God could add the pneuma, or the rational soul. This is the "feminine aspect of the Spirit" – the Greek term pneuma, often associated with the Holy Spirit of the New Testament. The Gnostics identified the Demiurge with the Jehovah of the Hebrews. In philosophy, the term is used to denote a Divine Being that is the builder of the universe rather than its creator." - Columbia Encyclopedia, Sixth Edition

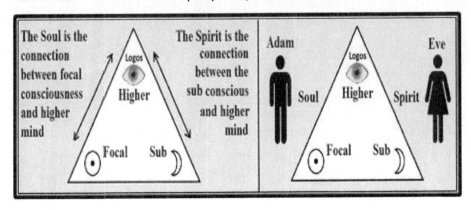

Terminal lucidity

Terminal lucidity or a rally before death usually occurs shortly before a person dies, and is noticeably pronounced in people with severe psychiatric or neurological disorders. Although, only seen in a minority of patients, those with conditions such as advanced Alzheimer's, schizophrenia, Parkinson's disease and tumours have been seen regaining mental clarity and memory for a short time before they die. Most of those who witness this event are confused as to what is taking place. The orthodox position within the mainstream medical profession assumes that human consciousness is the result of the physical construct of matter within the fabric of the brain and without such matter consciousness cannot exist. However, from a metaphysical perspective, the functioning arrangement of matter within the brain only acts as a receptive interface for consciousness to experience this physical reality.

Case 1: Anna Katharina Ehmer

In 1922, Anna Katharina Ehmer was a 26-year-old woman who lived in an institute for mental disorders in Hephata, a small town 50km south west of Kassel, German. She was one of the patients with the most severe mental disabilities and had not uttered a single word during her whole lifetime. She spent much of her time staring into space at a single spot or fidgeting for hours with a vacant expression. However, before she died, she was seen, by many staff members, singing songs for at least half an hour before she passed away.[1] One of the doctors Fredrich Happich recalls the event :

"One day I was called by one of our physicians, who is respected both as a scientist and a psychiatrist. He said: "Come immediately to Käthe, she is dying!" When we entered the room together, we did not believe our eyes and ears. Käthe, who had never spoken a single word, being entirely mentally disabled from birth on, sang dying songs to herself. Specifically, she sang over and over again, "Where does the soul find its home, its peace? Peace, peace,

heavenly peace!" For half an hour she sang. Her face, up to then so stultified, was transfigured and spiritualized. Then, she quietly passed away. Like myself and the nurse who had cared for her, the physician had tears in his eyes. We witnessed the dying of this girl with deepest emotions. Her death posed many questions to us. Obviously, Käthe had only superficially participated in all that happened in her surroundings. In reality, she had apparently internalized much of it. Because, where did she know the text and the melody of this song from, if not from her surroundings? Moreover, she had comprehended the contents of this song and used it appropriately in the most critical hour of her life. This appeared like a miracle to us."** - Fredrich Happich[2]

He also made the observation :

"Often in the last hours before death all pathological obstructions fell away and revealed an inner life of such beauty. That we could only stand in front of it, feeling shaken to the core." Fredrich Happich[3]

When viewing this case from the orthodox medical position it appears confusing. How is it possible for a dysfunctional brain to suddenly behave with purpose, perspective and clarity? As though a racing car whose engine had previously blown a head gasket, suddenly fires up on all cylinders to complete and win the race. But viewing it from the metaphysical position, it is easy to appreciate the subtle interaction between physical soul consciousness and eternal spirit consciousness. Where, during the changeover from life to death a subtle blending of the two positions of consciousness can occur. Furthermore, when we consider that the eternal spirit consciousness exists without the flawed constraints placed upon it by this physical realm and the limited physical body. Its unrestrained potential is far beyond our conceptual comprehension. This perfect unconstrained aspect of Käthe's consciousness momentarily integrated with her physical body resulting in the unusual lucid clarity of her true personality.

Case 2 : 1822, 6-year-old boy

In 1822 there was a published case in which a young boy of 6 fell on a nail, penetrating his forehead. By the age of 17 he had developed mental problems together with frequent headaches, leaving him in a state of melancholy, depression, pain and memory loss. He blinked continuously while looking at the same object for hours. Eventually, when he began to throw up frequently he was admitted to hospital. For 18 days he lay in the hospital bed unable to even sit up. However, on the 19th day he got out of his bed full of energy and enthusiasm claiming to be free from pain and all sickness, with a desire and expectation of leaving the hospital the very next day to go home. Fifteen minutes after the attending physician had left him, he fell unconscious only to die a few minutes later. At his autopsy two puss filled tissue bags the size of hen's eggs were found in the front part of his brain.[4]

Case 3 : Old Alzheimer's patient

A number of years ago an 81-year-old Icelandic lady developed Alzheimer's disease which left her demented during the final years of her life. Her family would take it in turns visiting her in the retirement home where she stayed. Although she had not been able to recognise any of them for at least a year prior to her death, one afternoon she sat up in bed and looked directly into the eyes of her son Lydur who was working on a crossword puzzle at the end of her bed, **"I'm going to recite a verse to you"** she said, clearly and loudly.

"Oh, father of light, be adored. Life and health, you gave to me, My father and my mother. Now I sit up, for the sun is shining. You send your light into me. Oh, God, how good you are." 81-year-old Icelandic lady[4]

After delivering the verse she lay back on her pillow and reverted back into the non-responsive state to which she was in before. A state which she stayed in until she died a few weeks later. Lydur, her son, thinking the verse was one of his mother's poems was surprise to find out it was actually a psalm written by a famous Icelandic poet.

The concept of the spiritual consciousness interfacing with the physical soul awareness during the final moments of one's life is simple enough to accept as a plausible explanation. However, the influence or interaction with spiritual consciousness months prior to an unexpected death places the paranormal aspect of this phenomena at another level. Some people believe that this world and our physical earthly experience is all part of a greater mechanism of overall conscious development and that our years here on this earth, as individuals, have purpose on many metaphysical levels. Consequently, times may arise when one's spiritual side of consciousness feels it necessary to intervene in this physical plane, in an attempt to alter or influence the direction and course of a person's life.

"Strange is our situation here on earth. Each of us comes for a short visit, not knowing why, yet sometimes seeming to divine a purpose." - Albert Einstein

"Each of us was born to fulfil a divine purpose. As we open our hearts and minds to a new way of being, the purpose of our lives unfolds organically." - Iyanla Vanzant

"You are here on earth for a divine purpose. It is not to be endlessly entertained or to be constantly in full pursuit of pleasure. You are here to be tried, to prove yourself so that you can receive the additional blessings God has for you. . . some blessings will be delivered in this life; others will come beyond the veil. The Lord is intent on your personal growth and development. That progress is accelerated when you willingly allow Him to lead you through every growth experience you encounter, whether initially it be to your individual liking or not." - Richard G. Scott

"Sometimes things aren't very clear, that's all. Things look like they're going against us, and though it always turns out fine in the end, and we can always look back and say oh of course it had to happen that

way, otherwise so-and-so wouldn't have happened - still while it's happening, in my heart I keep getting this terrible fear, this empty place, and it's very hard at such times really to believe in a plan with a shape bigger than I can see." - Thomas Pynchon, Gravity's Rainbow

"There comes a moment in life when you say to yourself - enough. This is ENOUGH! Then - you take a walk with your destiny. To change. To fulfil your purpose. We all have it. But are you willing to take that first step?" - Besa Kosova

"If you don't know where you're going, you'll end up someplace else." - Yogi Berra

"The most glorious moment you will ever experience in your life is when you look back and see how God was protecting you all this time." - Shannon L. Alder

"When you trust your inner guidance and begin moving in the direction of your dreams (aligned with your individual gifts) you will be cloaked in an armor bestowed upon you by your guardian angel." - Charles F. Glassman

"Sometimes we're persuaded to relinquish control, and when this happens, time becomes more synchronic and coincidence more profound. It's the same cosmic force, but without so many restrictions. This is when guardian angels can roll up their sleeves to say, 'Now we've got food and shelter done, let's get to work!'" - Jan Golembiewski, Magic

"You're on this earth with a divine purpose: to rise to the level of your highest creative possibility, expressing all that you are intellectually, emotionally, psychologically, and physically in order to make the universe a more beautiful place." - Marianne Williamson

"If there were no night, we would not appreciate the day, nor could we see the stars and the vastness of the heavens. We must partake of the bitter with the sweet. There is a divine purpose in the adversities we encounter every day. They prepare, they purge, they purify, and thus they bless." - James E. Faust

It is the belief of some that your life will not end until you have been given ample opportunities to fulfil your individual life's purpose. Furthermore, if, at any point in your life, you become locked within a cul-de-sac of day to day living, where necessary opportunities cannot penetrate, your spiritual subconscious could interfere upsetting the smooth running of your affairs in order to present new paths and opportunities through some extreme or drastic measure.

"If a window of opportunity appears, don't pull down the shade." - Tom Peters

"Sometimes whatever you think is killing you, might actually be resurrecting you." - Dr. Jacent Mpalyenkana, Ph.D. MBA

Because the spiritual side of our consciousness exists out of the physical constraints of time and space, from a vantage point where it is able to view past, present and future simultaneously, it is reasonable to assume that this aspect of our consciousness understands us better than we think we know ourselves, from our Earthly bound, soul vantage point. As a result, it could be beneficial to us if we tune into this part of our nature in order to help facilitate and fulfil our karmic and cosmic destiny.

There have been documented cases where people, who have died unexpectedly, have undertaken tasks, or said things, which are out of character to their normal routine, tasks or conversations which appear, to the onlooker, as trivial, but could very well be a necessary part of their karmic jigsaw before they move over to the next realm. Tasks which have all the hallmarks of spiritual guidance.

"A week before my father's fatal heart attack, he went out of his way to make amends with all of his brothers. Let's say they all didn't get along - He had seven. The last one he made amends with on Friday, my father died Friday night." - Καρδιά ενός [5]

The death of my own father

My own father, Richard Taylor, suffered an unexpected heart attack in September 2008. In the months leading to that day, he had been compiling, at least a dozen folders full of information for my mother and his family in the event he died suddenly. These folders turned out to be a major help for my mother who had to begin a new life as a widow. Furthermore, my parents had a lifelong pact with each other. Whoever died first would do what was necessary to contact the other. On the night of my father's death, I decided to move back into our family home, to help my mother cope with the grieving process. Although we were both mentally drained and neither of us could sleep, I persuaded my mum to go out with me for a walk, in an attempt at tiring us both out before bed. We walked and talked for over an hour or two before heading home. Although we still couldn't sleep, we felt like we had done something constructive towards dealing with our situation. Over the next few days, I tried to keep my mother occupied with things unrelated to my father's death, one of which was afternoon lunch with a friend in the next village. That afternoon, unknown to us, there was a promotional raffle where many local businesses, within the area, offered small prizes in an attempt to attract business. The hairdresser offered a free haircut, the butcher a free joint and the florist a free bunch of flowers. Each customer in the restaurant received a free raffle ticket with each meal. Unaware of my mother's new situation, we all sat down to eat a great lunch and thought no more of it. The next day my mum received a phone call from the restaurant telling her she had won a prize in the raffle. The prize she had won was an hour session with the local medium. Still keeping her affairs private, she called the medium and arranged to meet her over the next few days. By the time of the meeting, my mum, who had coped relatively well under her new circumstances, drove off to see the medium alone. After parking her car she knocked on the medium's door which opened to reveal a middle-aged lady who preceded to invite her in. As my mother walked into the sitting area, the medium said "**A man has just followed you through the door, who** has recently crossed over". After breaking down in tears for a moment my mother continued to hear what the lady wanted to tell her. Assuring her that my father was perfectly fine now and was sorry to have left so quickly. The medium said that my father was talking about a blue jumper (cardigan/sweatshirt) which my mother had placed under her pillow. It turned out to be the same blue jumper that my father would wear most days to work, which, after his death, my mother kept close to her at night. After an hour, fulfilling my father's part of the pact, my mother left the medium emotional but reassured that there is more to this life than just the normal day to day here and now.

Jean & Richard Taylor 1996

The spirit realm and our attachment to it can interact with this physical realm in many ways. It all depends upon how receptive the individual is who requires guidance or a helping hand. We all possess varying degrees of sensitivity within our five senses, allowing us to interface with this higher consciousness. Some people see spirits, some hear them and some even feel them. However, modern society is very much geared to the material aspect of life, giving little time or credence to our spiritual attachment, ultimately dulling the vast majority of people's sensual ability to benefit from this vast and limitless potential.

According to Sue Bishop, the author of *Psychic Kids,* most children possess psychic abilities, and that most people after the age of seven lose these abilities as the body matures and the brain splits into two independent hemispheres, prompting the ability to reason.

"It's when children go through this phase that they start to fear death and fear separation from a parent. They start to focus more on being logical and analytical. [...] They start to doubt their intuition, they shut that part of themselves off. [...] To keep sixth sense skills active children need to be reassured and not restrained." - Sue Bishop *(Psychic Kids)*

There have been accounts of people hearing, what appears to be, a voice, telling them to do something quick to avoid some kind of catastrophe.

Case 4 : Voice telling me to move

A married couple with a young son were moving from south Washington to the north. The wife and son drove in the family car while the husband took his old pickup. Along the way the husband's fuel pump gave up, so he sent his wife and son off to find a replacement, while he worked on the engine to remove the old pump by the side of the highway. Standing on the near side to the traffic he suddenly heard a voice close to his ear telling him "you're going to get hit". Because the voice came with authority, he immediately moved to the far side of the truck to continue work on the fuel pump.

"Sure, as shit, not more than two minutes later, another pickup comes down the on ramp at 50+ mph, broadsides my truck from the back bumper to the front. If I had stayed working on the pump, I'd have been turned into a jelly smear on the side of my truck." - Harry Palmer pick-up driver[6]

In another road accident case, a mystery voice came from nowhere to save a young lady who was caught up in a collision.

"My sister was in a car wreck and her '70s grocery-getter started flipping through the air. A voice loudly told her to lift her arms. She broke a bone in her hand, but she was told that doing that probably saved her life. Her hand took the brunt of the landing and she did not fall on her head." - Twotwirlygirlys[6]

In other cases, people have reported a sensation as though physical contact has been made by an unknown source which altered the outcome of a dangerous situation. And without this physical intervention their situation would not have turned out well.

Cases 5, 6 & 7 : A helping hand which came from nowhere

When Jackie was a young girl, she went with her family to the slopes of a popular sledding hill just after a fresh snow fall. Eager to have some fun she positioned herself at the top of the steepest part of the hill and began to descend with her eyes closed.

"I apparently hit someone going down and I was spinning out of control. I was heading for the metal guardrail. I didn't know what to do," says Jackie. "I suddenly felt something push my chest down. I came within less than a half inch of the rail but didn't hit it. I could have lost my nose." - Angel encounters[7]

Many years ago, a young female rock climber was attempting to climb up a shale rock face somewhere in the United States. When she was almost two thirds the way up, her left handhold broke free at the same moment she was reaching for her right handhold. At this point

13

everything appeared to be in slow motion as she could feel herself beginning to fall away from the entire rock face.

"I started to fall backwards and everything got real slow. I knew I was going to die or at best be crippled."

At this point she felt what seemed like a hand pressing against her shoulder blades, pushing her, once more, against the rock face and to safety.

"I took a moment to steady myself, I was pretty shaken up, and then I climbed down to safety. I am inclined to believe that it was a guardian angel, but that is solely based on my religious background." - Reedkeeper[6]

In 2004 the racing car driver Dale Earnhardt Jr wrecked his corvette in a practice session for an American Le Mans race series at Sonoma raceway. After what was a minor crash Earnhardt became dazed by the impact, leaving him in a semi-conscious state. During the crash the car's fuel connector split, spilling fuel all around the crash site which eventually ignited consuming most of the car and the surrounding area. In his semi-conscious state Earnhardt remembers someone pulling him out of the burning car by lifting him up under his arm pits and throwing him to safety.

"... I didn't get out. I don't have any memory of myself climbing out of the car. And I remember sort of moving, like in motion, like going to lean forward and try to climb out of the car, and then something grabbed me under the armpits, pulled me up over the door bars and then let go of me and I fell to the ground ..." - Dale Earnhardt Jr

Earnhardt woke up in hospital with second degree burns after a 12-hour morphine assisted sleep. The first thing he asked was who had helped pull him out of the car, only to be told he had climbed out all by himself. He replied by saying "bullshit".[8]

Dale Earnhardt Jr escapes burning car

Finally, we have cases of full-blown manifestations taking on human form, sometimes appearing out of nowhere, to assist or divert the recipient away from a dangerous or even fatal situation.

Cases 8,9 & 10 : I saw them standing there

In 1980 a single mother named Deb, living in Bernardino County, California, had just collected her two children from her parents' home 30 miles away. It was around 11:30pm and the traffic on the roads began to dwindle. Her old car had a faulty fuel gauge which left Deb guessing as to how much gas she had left in the tank. Half way home the car began to falter and Deb now realised she had run out of fuel.

"I pulled off the first off ramp I could, and it just happened to be one that was slightly uphill. Almost at the top of the exit, my car died and there was absolutely nothing around except empty fields and distant lights at a truck stop about a quarter of a mile down the road." - Deb

With no cars in sight Deb was at a loose end. These were the days before mobile phones, and the idea of carrying two small children miles in the dark was not a viable option.

"I put my head on the steering wheel while saying a short and panicky prayer," she says. "I hadn't even finished when I heard a few taps on my window." - Deb

When Deb looked up, she saw a young cleanly dressed and well-groomed man standing by her car. She recalled being extremely calm under circumstances which would have normally made her terrified. The man told her to put the car in neutral and he would help her over the small hill towards a place where she could find fuel.

"I thanked him and followed his instructions. The car started moving. I steered it toward the lights of the truck stop and turned around to yell 'thank you' again to him. [...] He was so nice! My car kept moving, but the young man was nowhere in sight. I mean, this area was completely remote. There was absolutely nowhere he could have gone that quickly, even if there was somewhere to go. I don't even know where he came from to begin with." - Deb

Deb's car rolled all the way down the hill, finally resting at a truck stop where she was able to refuel and drive her children home to safety.[7]

During times of war emotions and adrenalin run rampant, heightening the senses of those involved. Consequently, many accounts of paranormal activity and spiritual interventions have been documented. Accounts where soldiers have been saved by what some regard as guardian spirits or dead comrades.

In one account a Canadian Corporal by the name of Will Bird recalls one night in 1917 just after the battle of Vimy Ridge. He was sharing shelter with two other soldiers under a tarp near the front line, all of whom were getting some much-needed sleep.

"Before dawn, warm hands shook him. Wiping away sleep, he looked with amazement at his brother Steve, who had been reported

missing in action in 1915. Steve led him through some ruins, when he suddenly rounded a corner and disappeared." - Will Bird

Corporal Bird, still tired, settled down in his new location to grab more needed sleep, putting the sighting of his brother down to a hallucination brought on by his tiredness. However, in the morning he was stunned to learn about his two comrades who he previously shared a shelter with. Just before dawn they suffered a direct hit from a shell which dismembered them both beyond all recognition.[9]

In another story a Canadian soldier saw an apparition of his mother standing twenty yards from where he was carrying ammunition. As he scrambled towards the place where his mother appeared, he narrowly missed a direct hit from a German shell.

"One night while carrying bombs, I had occasion to take cover when about twenty yards off I saw you looking towards me as plain as life." Dumbstruck, he "crawled nearly to the place where your vision appeared" as a German shell slammed into the place he had just left behind. "Had it not been for you, I certainly would have been reported 'missing,'" the soldier wrote. "You'll turn up again, won't you, mother, next time a shell is coming?"[10]

Although the soul consciousness takes precedence here in the physical realm, during times of extreme trauma, it is possible that the spirit consciousness takes over detaching the individual's physical conscious perspective from a gruesome even painful experience.

Case 11 & 12 : I left my body

In the early 1970s Mike, the eldest son of Jasper Swain died in an auto-mobile accident in Kwazulu, Natal, South Africa. Mike who was only 18 at the time was travelling with Heather the 11-year-old daughter of a family friend. In the accident they were thought to have been killed instantly. After the funeral Jasper went to see Mrs Nina Merrington, a medium who was asked to make contact with Mike's spirit.

"After Nina passed into trance Jasper was startled to hear her speaking with Mike's voice, addressing him as 'Chud,' a name that only his dead son had ever used."

When questioned about the accident, Mike said he would allow Nina to relive the accident by placing her in the driving seat.

"It is a terribly hot day and I am driving along a very crowded road. There is a little girl beside me. Her name is Heather. She is chatting to me about her mum and dad, who are in the car ahead of us. I can see their car, approximately fifty yards away. It is grey in colour; it looks like a Rambler. It is noon and there is a mass of holiday traffic passing us in both directions." - "Now I see a black car coming towards us. As it approaches us, I see this other car coming behind it. I can see this other car clearly because it is in the middle of the road, trying to pass the black car."

The sun was glaring off the windscreen of the black car, which dazzled Mike and Heather's view as they approached. All of a sudden, the radiant glare changed from silver to gold as both Mike and Heather felt themselves being lifted up in the air, through the top of the car and out above the road.

"We have been lifted thirty feet above the Mini. And in one horrifying second, I see the little Mini and this large car collide head-on. There is a noise like the snapping of steel banjo strings. The little Mini bounces right off the highway, right over on to the gravel verge. It is finally brought to a halt in a cloud of dust when it hits a giant anthill."

As Mike and Heather looked down on the Mini, still holding each other's hands, they saw their crumpled bodies and realised they are now dead. They also describe how various people in glorious coloured clothes begin to gather around them; familiar faces of friends and loved ones who had previously passed over. All those who witnessed the medium contact Mike were reassured that they both passed over without experiencing fear, shock or suffering, as their conscious perspective shifted beyond the physical realm before the impact actually happened.[11]

Not all near-death experiences involve an actual accident, just the trauma associated with an expectation of death can be enough to separate the soul consciousness from the physical body.

A number of years ago a young man named Julian Milke and his mother were driving their car to a friend's house for dinner when his mother thought it would be a good idea to stop by the side of the road and pick some wild flowers for the occasion.

"She asked if I would stop the car and pick them as they would look nice on the dinner table. I pulled over to the right side of the road (it was not a major highway), parked the car, and went down a small incline to get off the road to pick the flowers. While I was picking the flowers, a car came whizzing by and suddenly headed straight for me. [...] As I looked up and saw what I presumed would be an inevitable death, I separated from my body and viewed what was happening from another perspective. My whole life flashed in front of me, from that moment backwards to segments of my life. The review was not like a judgement. It was passive, more like an interesting novelty." - Julian Milke (*Beyond the light.* P17)[12]

Although Julian had an out of the body, near-death experience, the speeding car finally veered away from hitting him and sped off as fast as it had appeared. While Julian suffered no injury, the sheer helpless terror involved seemed to be enough to promote his paranormal experience.

The word Angel comes from the Greek word 'angelos' which is derived from the Hebrew word 'malakh' meaning the one who is sent or the messenger. These angels are sent to occasionally guide us, through various means, towards pathways in life which help us fulfil our karmic goals. Early deaths are sometimes viewed as the completion of a karmic cycle or even a leap up onto another karmic level. It is also thought, in some spiritual circles, that people who pass away early in life often become spirit guides for the living.

Soul mates

Due to the spiritual aspect of our consciousness being outside the constraints of time and space, it has the ability to observe past, present and future events simultaneously, while at the same time interacting with other spiritual entities, in a form of collective. As a result, they are fully aware of all aspects of our Earthly bound soul consciousness, even better than we know ourselves. Consequently, when we meet another person, who we seem to have an immediate affinity or connection with, this could well be because we already know them on a spiritual level. These relationships are sometimes referred to as soul mates, unions which may very well have come together from some form of paranormal or spiritual intervention. Therefore, any person who neglects their spiritual side of consciousness, focusing entirely on their soul perspective and material matters will limit their overall potential within this earthly experience. Some people have great difficulty finding a soul mate. This could be because their lives are ordered in such a way as to leave no entry point for the soul mate to connect. Only when their rigid routine is broken or their pursuit of unnecessary objectives is diverted may the opportunity present itself.

When looking at the zodiac from the perspective of an average life of 72 years. The first half of the chart represents the physical years of the soul and focal consciousness while the second half represents the spiritual subconscious side of our nature.

Average life of 72 years

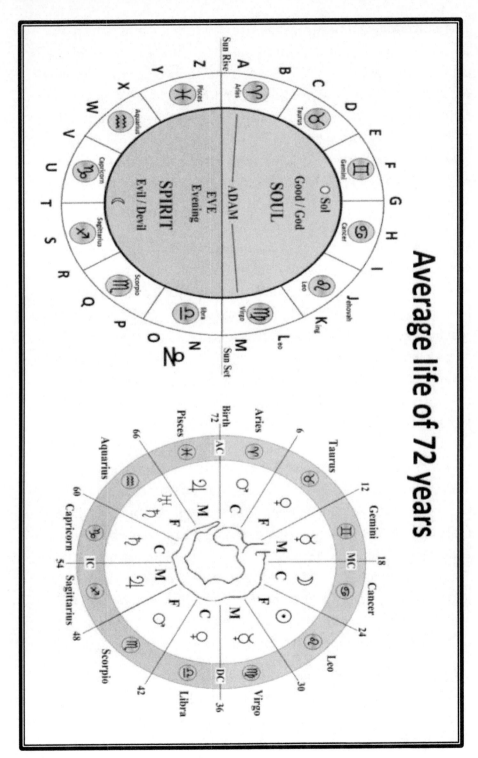

Cardinal, Fixed and Mutable Years

0 – 6 Cardinal : The beginning of life's journey.

6 – 12 Fixed : Fixed years of childhood.

12 – 18 Mutable : The change from child into adult.

18 – 24 Cardinal : The beginning of adulthood.

24 – 30 Fixed : Fixed years as a young adult.

30 – 36 Mutable : From young adult to middle age.

36 – 42 Cardinal : The beginning of Middle age.

42 – 48 Fixed : Fixed years of middle age.

48 – 54 Mutable : Change from middle to old age.

54 – 60 Cardinal : The beginning of old age.

60 – 66 Fixed : Fixed in old age.

66 – 72 Mutable : Change from this life to the next.

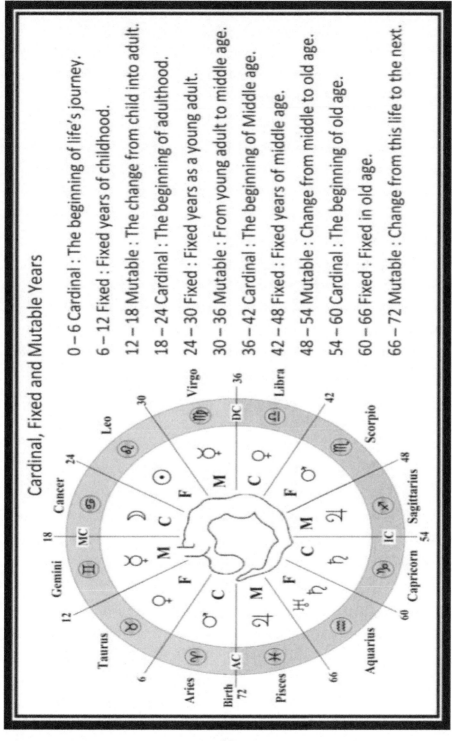

Birth – 6, Aries (I am), Mars (physical proactivity). The self, during these years, it is all about baby, which is all head, the size of which is out of proportion to the rest of its body. Baby has lots of proactive cardinal energy, he likes to explore his new world as he begins the journey through the first six signs of the zodiac.

6 – 12, Taurus (I have), Venus (love & liking). During these years the child learns about territorial boundaries and material possessions, he knows what toys are his and feels the need to make it clear to others. The child develops their own unique style of speech in order to interact and express themselves.

12 – 18, Gemini (I think), Mercury (communication). This is the house of communication and thinking, considered to be the most important years for learning and developing the life skills in order to communicate successfully. Gemini represents the twins, which could symbolise puberty, when the child changes into an adult. Mid heaven (MC), represents an individual's social identity, and a time when many decide their career path.

18 – 24, Cancer (I feel), Moon (internal emotion). These were traditionally the years when one would enter into a serious loving, emotional relationship, possibly leading to marriage. Cancer is also the 4th house of home, a time when many people would move away from their parents to set up home for themselves.

24 – 30, Leo (I will), Sun (self). This is the optimum period when people shine their individual uniqueness and focused willpower out into the world. They are in their prime with good vitality. A good time for setting the foundations for a new career, business or way of life.

30 – 36, Virgo (I examine), Mercury. These are the years of examination, service to others and health. DC. This is our relationship identity, most people, by this stage in their lives, are established in some form of relationship, their identity is generally shaped by it.

36 – 42, Libra (I complement), Venus. These are the balancing scales in which we go from the top half, the masculine side of the chart, to the bottom, feminine side. They say life begins at 40, it certainly does for many people, their ego becomes diluted in favour of a more balanced view of life, this is essentially because they are beginning to experience their surroundings from a spiritual perspective too. At this point most people have developed enough social skills to function comfortably, complimenting their environment. Consequently, many people have a greater appreciation of what makes them tick, they don't necessarily know for sure what they want from life, but they have a better idea of what they don't want.

42 – 48, Scorpio (I desire), Mars, the house of sex and transformation. Sometimes called the frustrating 40s, many males harbour the desire to pursue an affair, some go along with it, releasing themselves from their mundane stale relationships. It is the average age for a man to divorce.[13] Men get to a certain age where they see themselves getting old, and feel the need for a final fandango before they resign themselves to being over the hill.

48 – 54, Sagittarius (I seek), Jupiter (expansion). This is the house of travel, higher learning and philosophy. After most people have come to terms with the loss of their youth and their sexual appetite, many evolve towards the next natural progression of the 9th house. At this time many people seek deep meaningful, philosophical answers to life's bigger questions, along with an interest in long distance travel.

54 – 60, Capricorn (I use), Saturn, which rules time, also known as Cronus, is a period in which time becomes an issue. Most people start to appreciate their own mortality, realising that their time in the physical body is now limited. Capricorn also rules the 9th house of career. For most men these are the years of peak responsibility along with peak earnings.

60 – 66, Aquarius (I know), Saturn and Uranus. This is a period in which life's accumulated experiences offer a mature sense of knowing. If one

has followed their karmic path over social pressures and temptations, the rewards should manifest a harmonious and balanced temperament, leading to feelings of peace and fulfilment. The second half of this sign is ruled by Uranus, a planet synonymous with freedom, this coincides with most people's retirement age.

66 – 72, Pisces (I believe), Jupiter. These are the final years of most people's lives, where they reflect and put everything in perspective. Here they have time to question their own beliefs and traditional values. Many turn to some form of spiritual or philosophical belief as a comforting stepping stone towards their transition into the next realm.

Midlife crisis

Many people go through, what some call, a midlife crisis. It is a period in a person's life when they reflect and reassess the overall direction and purpose of their lives, bringing to the surface deep feelings and emotions concerning a variety of issues and aspects of their lives. When using the zodiac as a benchmark for an average life of 72 years, we can see that around the age of 36 a person enters the sign of Libra, the sign of the balancing scales. Here they move into the second half of the chart promoting their spiritual side as opposed to the first 36 years of focal conscious awareness which underpinned the ego as they explored the world from a predominantly physical perspective. When the spiritual subconscious kicks in, it promotes more of an inward perspective, feelings of reflection and re-evaluation towards their life's expectations and overall purpose. Their inner voice begins to question the path they find themselves on, leading many to make dramatic changes in relation to the direction their lives are taking. The inner voice is your intuition, it is your gut feeling and your main guardian. The German word for God is 'Gott' a similar pronunciation to the English word 'gut'. During this time an individual may find that their subconscious purposely propels them into undertaking illogical or out of character scenarios, sometimes resulting in life changing consequences.

Some people believe that this world and our physical earthly experience is part of a greater mechanism of conscious development and that our years on this earth have purpose on many metaphysical levels. Consequently, if your life requires a change of direction towards a deeper spiritual perspective, it can be interesting to see how the conscious universe will appear to conspire around you in such a way as to make your new path seem relatively easy. People, places and situations will appear to unfold in a synchronised manner giving your new path an attractive yet paranormal dimension.

"To realise one's destiny is a person's only real obligation. All things are one. When you want something all the universe conspires in helping you to achieve it." - Paulo Coelho

Notes for chapter 1

(1) Nahm M, Greyson B. The death of Anna Katharina Ehmer: a case study in terminal lucidity. NCBI.
https://www.ncbi.nlm.nih.gov/pubmed/24547666

(2) Terminal lucidity: the researchers attempting to prove your mind lives on even after you die. Mel Magazine.
https://melmagazine.com/en-us/story/terminal-lucidity-the-researchers-attempting-to-prove-your-mind-lives-on-even-after-you-die

(3) Trost, M. (1983). Friedrich Happich. Self-published booklet.
https://pdfs.semanticscholar.org/8315/9e3e4eb76af669d3636afe7b44fc2a65f394.pdf

(4) Michael Nahm a , Bruce Greyson a, *, Emily Williams Kelly a , Erlendur Haraldsson. Terminal lucidity: A review and a case collection. Archives of Gerontology and Geriatrics.
file:///C:/Users/btayl/OneDrive/Documents/Downloads/Nahmetal_TerminalLucidity_AGG.pdf

(5) Καρδιά ενός, Unexplained mysteries.com, 2008.
https://www.unexplained-mysteries.com/forum/topic/118707-can-people-sense-death/

(6) Melissa Brinks, 15 People Tell Eerie Stories Of Guardian Angels Looking Out For Them.
https://www.ranker.com/list/reddit-true-stories-of-guardian-angels/melissa-brinks

(7) Stephen Wagner, 10 true stories of Angel encounters, 2018,
https://www.liveabout.com/angel-encounters-true-stories-2593644

(8) Gary Gustely, Dale Earnhardt Jr. says a ghost saved his life, but Bigfoot isn't real. Fox News. 2018.
https://www.foxnews.com/auto/dale-earnhardt-jr-says-a-ghost-saved-his-life-but-bigfoot-isnt-real

(9) Will R Bird, Ghosts Have Warm Hands: A Memoir of the Great War, 1916-1919.
https://www.amazon.com/Ghosts-Have-Warm-Hands-1916-1919/dp/1896979009

(10) Canadian soldiers embraced the 'supernatural, uncanny and ghostly' on the front lines, historian says. National Post, 2013.
https://nationalpost.com/news/world/canadian-soldiers-embraced-the-supernatural-uncanny-and-ghostly-on-the-front-lines-historian-says

(11) Jasper Swain, On the death of my son: An account of life after death.
https://www.amazon.com/Death-My-Son-Account-After/dp/0850307880

(12) P M H Atwater, Beyond the light, near-death experience. 1995, page 17.
https://www.amazon.com/Beyond-Light-Death-Experience-Story/dp/1855385104

(13) Tash Bell, Divorce in middle age: Can your marriage survive the 'frustrated forties'?, The Telegraph, 2015,
http://www.telegraph.co.uk/women/sex/relationship-advice-and-romance/11773012/Divorce-in-middle-age-Can-your-marriage-survive-the-frustrated-forties.html

Chapter 2. Animals and pets

"These special creatures appear in our lives for a purpose and at a specific time. Although their appearance may be different from the last time, they were with you, you may recognise something familiar about their personality, and you may sense a bond immediately as you look in their eyes. Look closely when a new pet comes into your life, and you will know." - Claire Montanaro (The Spiritual Life of Pets and other Animals).[1]

Some people believe that animals also have a connection to the spirit realm, and that certain pets which join us during various periods in our lives are part of our spiritual network, returning time and again throughout our many physical experiences and incarnations. These soul pets or guardian spirits will invariably seek you out, at a point in your life when you subconsciously truly need them.

Herd animals, such as cows and sheep, are thought to share a common soul, like a hive type of awareness, due to their basic evolutionary level. Consequently, it is assumed that they do not possess an established connection to what we would consider as spiritual consciousness.

Then God said, "Let us make man in our image, after our likeness. And let them have dominion over the fish of the sea and over the birds of the heavens and over the livestock and over all the earth and over every creeping thing that creeps on the earth." - Genesis 1:26 (ESV)

This verse from Genesis talks about giving man dominion over the livestock and all things which creep on the Earth. Pets are not normally considered as livestock, and therefore have more of an advanced form of consciousness than the wild or herd animals mentioned in Genesis. This could be due to their unique and more sophisticated connection to the spirit world, and as a consequence, we treat them more favourably than the animals we have dominion over, that is, the ones which are generally reared for consumption.

Evidence for the domestication of dogs as pets and companions goes back at least 12,000 years. The ancient temple of Gobekli Tepe, in Turkey, is a recent discovery, proving human culture and social structures existed all those years ago, showing evidence which points to the domestication of dogs.[2] In ancient Persia, dogs were said to guard the bridge between this world and the next, and depending upon how one treated their dog would influence their chances of reaching paradise (beyond the divide). Persian dogs, throughout this period, were thought to have souls, made up of 1/3 wild animal, 1/3 human and 1/3 divine. As a result, they were given their own funerals, sometimes equal in status to that of humans. They also had a tradition in which dogs would be brought close to a newly deceased person due to their superior sensors for some form of practical or spiritual reasons.[2]

In the old Indian epic known as 'Mahabharata', (400 BC), King Yadisthira makes a pilgrimage to his final resting place. Along the way, he was accompanied by his family and his faithful dog. One by one the members of his family died off leaving him and his dog alone. When the king reached the gates of heaven, he was welcomed in for all the noble and righteous things he had done throughout his life. However, the angel at the gate told him that his dog was not allowed inside. Devastated by this news, the king chose to remain with his dog, on Earth or even in hell, as opposed to paradise separated from his faithful friend. Before Yadisthira left, the angel told him that he had just passed the final test of his virtue and of course the dog was welcome inside, to stay with him in paradise. In some versions of this story the dog turns out to be Vishnu, the preserver, who had been watching over Yadisthira throughout his entire life, linking the figure of the dog to divinity.

Many ancient civilisations and cultures treated dogs with similar regard. Records from China suggest that their ancestors saw the dog as a gift from the heavens, which gave them an elevated status. Consequently, their blood was often used to seal oaths and allegiances. Dogs were sacrificed and buried in front of one's house or even at the city gates as a way to ward off evil spirits and protect those living within the city walls from bad luck and disease.

The Mayan and Aztec cultures have a similar belief regarding their dogs. Believing that they could help a recently deceased soul navigate its way into paradise. Any soul which died alone, receiving no proper burial, would be found by spirit dogs who would lead them to where they needed to go. Some Mesoamerican cultures tell of a time when dogs were instrumental in the destruction of an ungrateful and unknowing race of humans, which the Gods first created but later regretted. They say that because dogs have been here longer than this present race of humans, they were treated with the same amount of respect as the elders in their society.

In ancient Egypt the dog was linked to the jackal God Anubis, a figure who would guide the newly deceased to the hall of truth, a place where their soul would be judged by the great God Osiris. Wealthy Egyptian families would have their dogs mummified after death along with an elegant burial service.

The Greeks, who also domesticated their dogs, saw them as companions, protectors and hunting aids, they introduced the spiked collar as a way of shielding the dog from preying wolves. Socrates claimed in Plato's *Republic* that the dog was a true philosopher :

"And surely this instinct of the dog is very charming;--your dog is a true philosopher. Why, because he distinguishes the face of a friend and of an enemy only by the criterion of knowing and not knowing. And must not an animal be a lover of learning who determines what he likes and dislikes by the test of knowledge and ignorance?" - Plato's Republic Book II [3]

Therefore, the dog has learned who is a friend and who is foe, based on the simple knowledge of truth, whereas humans are often deceived as to who their true friends are due to hidden motives and agendas.

Cerberus was a Greek mythological three headed dog who guarded the gates of Hades, also known as the hound of hades, his role was to prevent the dead from leaving.

Cerberus

Argos, another famous Greek dog, was the loyal companion of King Odysseus of Ithaca, from Homer's book *Odyssey* (800 BC). In the story, King Odysseus returned home after 20 years, unrecognised by his wife and her entourage of suitors, who while trying to gain her hand in marriage, became hostile towards Odysseus, unsure of who he was and what his motives were. In spite of this hostility, his loyal dog Argos did recognise his master and rose up from the spot where he had been faithfully waiting for 20 years. Unable to give away his disguise, Odysseus ignored his old friend who, as a result, lay back down and died. This story expresses the unwavering devotion a dog has towards his master, no matter how long they have been apart.

In ancient Greece, there was a school of philosophers known as Cynics. These cynics tried to live a life of virtue, in harmony with nature, by rejecting all conventional desires for material wealth, power and fame. They would lead a simple life, on a day to day basis, free from social toils and unnecessary possessions. The first philosopher to outline these concepts was a pupil of Socrates by the name of Antisthenes, back in the late 5th century BC. He was followed by an extreme cynic called Diogenes who lived in a ceramic jar out on the streets of Athens. Following on from Diogenes was Crates of Thebes, a man who gave away a large personal fortune to live the life of an Athenian cynic, in abject poverty.

The name cynic is derived from the ancient Greek word 'Kynikos' which translates into 'dog like'. This name was given to the first cynic philosophers partly because Antisthenes taught his initial concepts in the Cynosarges (place of the white dog) gymnasium in Athens. It is also believed that the term dog was used to describe these people as an insult for their life style and rejection of conventional manners, choosing instead to live like dogs on the streets of Athens. Diogenes was often referred to as a dog. The modern interpretation of the term cynicism has evolved from the negative aspects of this ideology, drawing from its disbelief in the sincerity or goodness of human motives and actions.

Dogs in Rome were viewed in much the same way as they were in Greece, very much appreciated as guardians of the home.

"Never, with them on guard, need you fear for your stalls a midnight thief, or onslaught of wolves, or Iberian brigands at your back" - Virgil, Georgics III 404ff

The Roman Goddess Trivia (Roman version of the Greek Hecate) was the queen of ghosts, who haunted cross roads and grave yards, together with an association with witchcraft. A dog who seemingly barked away at nothing was thought to be warning those around them against the approach of Trivia or some other malevolent spirit.

Dog's senses

Dogs possess senses far superior to those of humans, giving them a greater depth and perception of the environment in which they occupy.

While humans try to rationalise, judge and even deny some of their own senses dogs do not, they react in a pure and unbiased manner according to what is going on around them.

"If you observe a dog standing in the corner, barking at nothing visible, then there's a pretty good chance that he's barking at an entity, spirit, or energy that doesn't belong there." - Marti Miller, pet psychologist

Dogs have over 100 million olfactory sensory receptors in their nose compared to humans who have only 6 million. Furthermore, the part of their brain responsible for processing odours is around 40 times larger than ours. It is therefore estimated that dogs, in general, can smell 1,000 to 10,000 times greater than we do. The dog's nostrils work independently from each other, allowing them to quickly establish the direction of scent. The air passageways at the end of the nose direct air leaving from mixing too much with the air entering, preserving the integrity of the initial scent. The dog's nasal tissues are arranged in such a way as to channel 12% of that air into a separate area at the back of its nose trapping and mixing that air with the dog's mucus, allowing further analysis of the scent's chemical make up.[4]

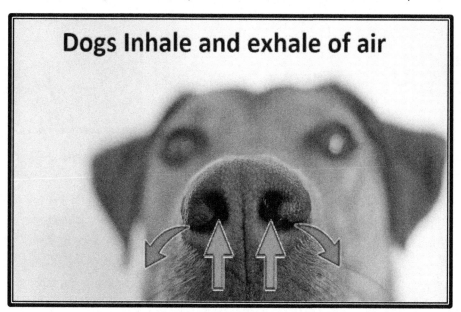

Dogs Inhale and exhale of air

Due to the dogs advanced sense of smell, humans have trained them to help locate missing people, dead bodies, drugs and explosives together with sniffing out tumours and helping the blind.

Together with a superior sense of smell, many dogs have impressive hearing. With three times the number of muscles in the outer ear, they are able to rotate their ears towards any noise funnelling the sound towards their inner ear. With a longer ear canal, the muscles help to process the sound in such a way as to give them greater sensitivity in pitch and volume. While humans are only able to hear sounds between 20hz and 20,000hz a dog's range is far greater at between 67hz to 45,000hz. Furthermore, they have the ability to hear these frequencies at a reduced volume.[5]

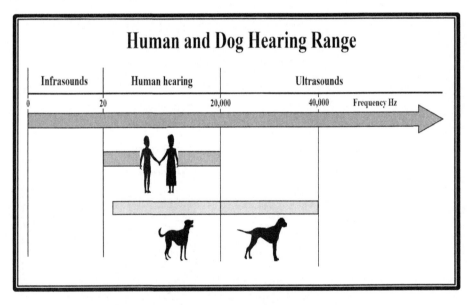

While human eyes look straight forward the average dog's eyes are set at an approximate angle of 20 degrees. While this increases their field of vision, they lose out on their binocular perspective when it comes to detail. Having only 1/10 the cone receptors of a human eye, the dog's retina is geared more towards motion with greater sensitivity in dim lighting at the expense of colour perception and clarity. New evidence suggests that they only see variations of blues, yellows and greys, allowing 61% more ultra violet light to pass onto their retinas, giving them greater scope within the ultraviolet range. Most dogs have what is referred to as 20/75 vision, meaning they can identify an object at 20 feet which we humans can see clearly at 75. However, some breeds of Labrador are bred with almost 20/20 vision, many of which are used as guide dogs for the blind.[6]

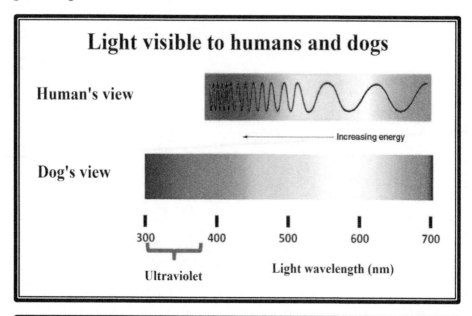

Light visible to humans and dogs

Human's view

Increasing energy

Dog's view

300 400 500 600 700

Ultraviolet

Light wavelength (nm)

When a dog looks in the mirror does he see the face of God?

Our perception of reality within this physical realm is formed from the detectable scope within our senses. As humans, our five senses are relatively modest almost handicapping us with limited capacity at detecting various forms and expressions of energy occupying the space within our surroundings.

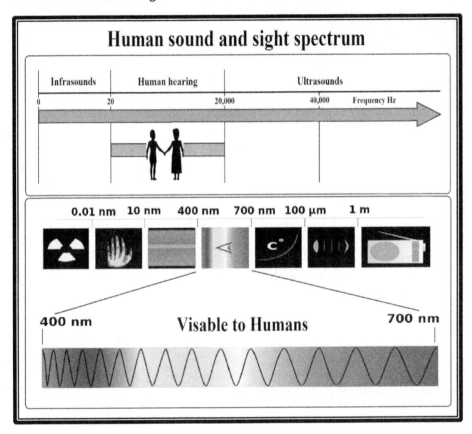

It is therefore plausible to assume that expressions of conscious energy which our sensory range fail to detect, does not necessarily mean that these energies do not exist. However, dogs with a superior range of detectability could very well pick up on energies we, as humans, are unaware of. It is believed by many spiritualist and esoteric wisdom seekers that human consciousness exists outside the biological vessel of the human body; An independent form of energy where our consciousness or point of attention separates from the body on death, releasing it back into its natural state within the higher vibrational frequency ranges associated with the spirit realm, essentially to become spirits or light beings. Hence why, in our ancient past and traditional cultures, it was believed that the dog had the ability to interface with the fringes of these higher frequency realms connected to the afterlife.

In the book *'Tails of the afterlife'* by Peggy Schmidt, she gives multiple accounts of unexplainable actions taken by various dogs who apparently interact with what can only be described as unseen entities or spirits. In one account she mentions a lady by the name of Del Johnson who died suddenly leaving six cats and seven dogs. Many believe that Mrs Johnson still visits her pets daily. Eye witness reports tell of seeing her animals suddenly gather in one spot. Furthermore, the dogs would wag their tails and flop over for a belly rub, while the cats arched their backs and purred. The animals would all sit to attention while staring into the air as though they were with some form of conscious energy giving them a great deal of attention.[7]

In the 1999 book *'Dogs that know when their owners are coming home and other unexplained powers of animals: An investigation,'* Rupert Sheldrake, concludes :

"There is a strong connection between humans and animals that defies present-day scientific understanding." - Rupert Sheldrake [8]

"The number one clue that there's something present is that your pet will stare up into the corner of a room at nothing," Anderson says. **"Upper corners of rooms are energy vortexes. Energy collects there like a dust bunny under your couch. So, you'll see the pet staring up in the corner, or your dog will look up and start barking."** - **"Pets might also act really weird,"** Anderson says. **"They won't go into a certain bedroom, or they won't go into a basement. I hear that a lot!"** - Karen Anderson, a professional animal communicator, psychic and medium.[9]

Both wild and domestic animals have been seen acting strangely before earthquakes and tsunamis. During the Boxing Day Indian Ocean earthquake and tsunami of 2004, dogs were seen to display distress with a change in behaviour before humans noticed anything unusual. Dogs were seen barking excessively, running for cover or refusing to go outside many minutes before the visible effects became apparent. Experts have suggested that some dogs can sense the Earth's vibrational changes before we humans can.

Black dog is a term used which generally refers to a demonic entity found throughout European and British folklore. These black dogs are described as nocturnal apparitions or even shape shifters associated with death, the underworld and even the Devil himself. While the vast majority of these myths and tales portray these black dogs as malevolent and sinister creatures, a few cases refer to them as benevolent, acting more like guardian angels in dog form, guiding travellers on the right path or guarding them from unwanted danger.

Dartmoor is an area of English moorland in southern Devon, notorious for black dog and hound stories. During the 17th century, a squire and huntsman by the name of Richard Cabell was said to have sold his soul to the Devil. Consequently, after his death, in 1677, black hounds began to appear around his burial chamber. On occasions, his ghostly apparition was reported riding the moors with a pack of black hunting dogs. This folklore tale was the inspiration behind Arthur Conan Doyle's famous book 'The Hound of the Baskervilles'.[10]

A few years ago a young mother living in New York told her story of how a golden retriever appeared out of nowhere to save her baby son's life. At the time, she was living in an apartment near Central Park where she would take her baby boy for daily exercise. On this particular day she decided to venture further afield towards the Metropolitan Museum of Art. After a pleasant walk around the museum grounds, she chose a nice spot to rest and take in the view at the top of a grassy hill overlooking 85th Street, where she could watch the people playing in the park together with the cars on the street down below.

"I'll never know exactly what happened. Did I look away for a moment after I unbuckled his seat belt. Did Jon see something that attracted him? In the space of a second, life can change; and somehow, suddenly, there was Jon running down the steep hill. I ran after him, vaguely aware that other people started running as well. He seemed to gain momentum and was hurtling down the hill so quickly, I knew I'd never be able to catch him. I also knew (as did the other people running with me) that if Jon couldn't stop, he would plunge headlong into the street. There were no barriers to stop him. The cars kept driving and Jon just kept running toward them." - Jon's mother [11]

Suddenly, out of nowhere, appeared a huge golden retriever, which ran past the panic stuck mother, down the hill, towards the baby boy. Once in front of the boy, the dog turned, placing himself directly in front of the boy's path. The baby careered into the dog, cushioned by its fury body and fell to the ground unscathed, saved from what seemed as impending doom.

"People surrounded us and cheered. I soon found the dog's owner. "Your dog saved my son," I gasped. "Another few seconds and he would have landed in the street." - "Kane is a good boy," she answered." - Miracle on 85th street.[11]

Saint John Bosco

Saint John Bosco (1815 - 1888) was an Italian Roman Catholic Priest, who dedicated his life towards helping street children, juvenile delinquents and various other forms of disadvantaged youth. At that time parts of Turin, in northern Italy, were considered too dangerous to walk at night. However, on occasions Bosco had to work late and found it necessary to cross through this dangerous district to get home. One night as he was just about to enter the Valdocco neighbourhood, a large grey dog appeared, almost from nowhere. Startled at first, he later found the dog to be a friendly companion and was happy to accept his company. As they both proceeded through the streets of this uninviting quarter the priest gave the dog the name Grigio (grey in Italian). As the weeks went by this became a regular occurrence, whenever Bosco was out late, needing to traverse through the hazardous part of town this large grey dog would appear to escort him. One night Bosco noticed two men behaving suspiciously as they appeared to follow him. Whenever he sped up or slowed down they would do the same. When he tried to lose them by crossing the road, they caught up with him, threw a cloak over his head, pinned him to the ground and forced a handkerchief into his mouth. As he struggled and called for help, he froze at the sound of a blood curdling howl which came from Grigio, who appeared at the nick of time to pounce on the two men knocking them both to the ground while digging his snarling teeth into their flesh. Terrified they both ran off leaving Bosco shaken but unscathed. Over the years the dog saved the priest from numerous ordeals. On one occasion, he even lay across the entrance of his doorway growling to prevent him from leaving his home. This action saved him from grave danger as two men were waiting down the road to rob and attack the priest. The last time John Bosco saw Grigio was on a journey to a friends house. It was getting dark and he had already passed a number of farms and vineyards guarded by dogs of various kinds. At that moment he thought of Grigio and wished the dog was with him. Almost instantaneously the dog appeared and began to accompany him on his walk. This turned out to be a lucky escape for Bosco, because moments later two aggressive farm dogs came running towards him growling and barking menacingly. However, with one all mighty howl from Grigio, the dogs scattered and ran back quickly in the direction from which they came. Grigio escorted Bosco to his friend's house where he lay by the priest's side while they ate. After supper the dog disappeared never to be seen again.

"So how can the incredible timing and actions of "Grigio" the stray dog be explained? How is it that he mysteriously showed up at just the right moment on not one, but numerous occasions to literally save the life of Father John Bosco? Was Grigio an Angel in the form of a dog? Or was he simply a dog that was mysteriously guided by God

to protect Don Bosco?" - St. John Bosco and the mysterious dog who protected him.[12]

Many people, throughout history, have pondered on the question whether or not animals go to heaven. To answer this question it is necessary to understand what form our consciousness takes in the afterlife and whether certain animals have the potential to interact with that conscious energy once outside this physical realm.

"For what happens to the children of man and what happens to the beasts is the same; as one dies, so dies the other. They all have the

same breath, and man has no advantage over the beasts, for all is vanity. All go to one place. All are from the dust, and to dust all return. Who knows whether the spirit of man goes upward and the spirit of the beast goes down into the earth?" -   Ecclesiastes 3:19 -21 (ESV)

As we have previously discussed, according to the Bible, man was made in the image of God and to his likeness. With dominion over the animals of the Earth.

Then God said, "Let us make man in our image, after our likeness. And let them have dominion over the fish of the sea and over the birds of the heavens and over the livestock and over all the earth and over every creeping thing that creeps on the earth." - Genesis 1:26 (ESV)

Man was given an essence of divine spark, an eternal spiritual attachment to the Creator. Separating and elevating him from the rest of the animal kingdom, enabling him, through his unique and advanced form of consciousness, to fashion the Earth as it is in heaven. This is essentially the spiritual aspect of consciousness influencing the collective soul consciousness within this physical realm. However, the soul is our earth bound point of attention reliant upon the five senses in order to formulate a rational perception of this physical reality. When the body ages and finally gives up the day to day battle for life, our consciousness or point of attention separates reverting back into its spirit form, from which it initially came, independent from the earthly constraints of space and time. Whether or not animals have this divine spark or spirit connection is a matter of subjectivity.

Then the LORD said, "My Spirit will not remain with man forever, because he is also flesh; nevertheless his days shall be 120 years." - Genesis 6 : 3 (NASB)

The word 'animal' is interesting in its own right, as the word could be viewed as 'ani', to animate, and 'mal' which derives from the Latin meaning bad, evil or wrongly. While this description applies to a number of wild animals it most certainly does not reflect the majority of family pets, who appear to possess a more advanced form of consciousness, closer to that of humans as opposed to the beasts found out in the fields, which are regarded, by some, as animated evil.

Although the soul is regarded by many as a mechanism to connect with divine essence, this could very well be misunderstanding the basic difference between spirit and soul consciousness, viewing the soul as spirit and visa versa. Furthermore, while all of God's creatures possess animated soul consciousness, many of them may not possess the divine spark of spirit which makes humanity different. Most humans have a sophisticated combination of conscious perspectives placing them above all the animals, a conscious awareness fashioned in the image of God.

"Hinduism also outlines a type of reincarnation, in which a being's eternal soul, or jiva, is reborn on a different plane after death, continuing until the soul is liberated (moksha). Animals have souls, but most Hindu scholars say that animal souls evolve into the human plane during the reincarnation process. So, yes, animals are a part of the same life-death-rebirth cycle that humans are in, but at some point they cease to be animals and their souls enter human bodies so they can be closer to God." - Adam Epstein[13]

"Buddhism says that among the realms a being can be reborn into, there are several "heavens," though they are not permanent places. Eventually the cycle begins again and one is reborn into another place, and this continues until Nirvana. Buddhism also sees animals as sentient beings like humans, and says that humans can be reborn as animals and animals can be reborn as humans. So given that, the question of whether or not animals can go to heaven doesn't really apply to Buddhists. Humans and animals are all interconnected." - Adam Epstein[13]

"Not every beast has a soul that goes to heaven. However, there are higher level beings and low level beings. Ants, for example, I'm

confident don't die and go to heaven to live eternity in bliss. Smack a mosquito... sorry, it's not going to be going to heaven to live a wonderful eternity. The truth is, there are specific differentiations with animals. All animals that have compassion to humans have a soul. The bottom line is this: if the animal had an emotional connection with you, then I can assure you.. they are on the other side." - Blair Robertson, Psychic Medium.[14]

Notes for chapter 2

(1) Claire Montanaro, The Spiritual Life of Pets and other Animals. Inlumino Global, https://www.inluminoglobal.com/articles/spiritual-life-pets-and-animals/

(2) Joshua J Mark. Dogs in the Ancient world. 2019. Ancient History Encyclopedia. https://www.ancient.eu/article/184/dogs-in-the-ancient-world/

(3) The Republic, Book II, Plato. The Literature Page, http://www.literaturepage.com/read/therepublic-81.html

(4) A Dog's sense of smell, Science netlinks, http://sciencenetlinks.com/daily-content/9/25/

(5) Eileen Anderson, How Does Dogs' Hearing Compare To Humans'?, Eileenanddogs, 2019, https://eileenanddogs.com/blog/2019/03/21/dogs-hearing-vs-human-hearing/

(6) Stanley Coren Phd, Can dogs see in ultraviolet?, Psychology Today, 2016, https://www.psychologytoday.com/us/blog/canine-corner/201604/can-dogs-see-in-ultraviolet

(7) Peggy Schmidt, Tails of the Afterlife: True Stories of Ghost Pets. 2009, ISBN-10 : 0764332538. https://www.amazon.com/Tails-Afterlife-True-Stories-Ghost/dp/0764332538

(8) Rupert Sheldrake, Dogs that know when their owners are coming home and other unexplained powers of animals: An investigation, https://www.amazon.com/Dogs-That-Their-Owners-Coming/dp/0307885968

(9) Wendy Wilson, Caitlin Ultimo, Boo! Can Dogs See Ghosts?, Bechewy, 2017,

https://be.chewy.com/behavior-pet-facts-can-pets-see-ghosts-6-behaviors-to-watch-for/

(10) Black Dog, wikipedia.
https://en.wikipedia.org/wiki/Black_dog_(ghost)

(11) Lynn Lowin, Miracle on 85th street, How a huge dog saved my child's life.
https://www.goodnewsnetwork.org/miracle-on-eighty-fifth-street-is-about-how-a-huge-dog-saved-my-childs-life/

(12) Geoff Heggadon, St. John Bosco and the mysterious dog who protected him. Works by Faith Ministries. 2014.
http://www.worksbyfaith.org/st-john-bosco-and-the-mysterious-dog-who-protected-him/

(13) Adam Epstine, Pope Francis says all pets go to heaven, but what do other religions say?, Quartz, 2014.
https://qz.com/311346/pope-francis-says-all-pets-go-to-heaven-but-what-do-other-religions-say/#:~:text=Hinduism%20also%20outlines%20a%20type,plane%20during%20the%20reincarnation%20process.

(14) Blair Robertson, Psychic Medium, Do pets go to heaven. Blog.
https://blairrobertson.com/blog/do-pets-go-to-heaven/

Chapter 3. Reincarnation

Reincarnation : Also called transmigration or metempsychosis, in religion and philosophy, rebirth of the aspect of an individual that persists after bodily death—whether it be consciousness, mind, the soul, or some other entity—in one or more successive existences.
- Britannica definition

The term reincarnation comes from the Latin which literally means 'entering the flesh again'. The concept of the soul, mind or consciousness continuing after death, to be reborn in cycles throughout various lifetimes is an old one. It seems the older the religion or philosophy the greater chance in its belief. The Greek equivalent to this concept is called metempsychosis, which is derived from two words meta (beyond) and empsykhoun which means 'to put a soul into'.

While some Jewish scholars vigorously reject the whole notion of reincarnation, many kabbalists embrace it as an underlining principle within their mystical sect. This concept within Judaism was thought to have originated around the same time as the Golden Age of Islam and the formation of the House of Wisdom during the 8th century. Rare books and scrolls were collected from all over the known world to be translated into Arabic by both Islamic and Judaic scholars searching for truth, enlightenment and wisdom. Manuscripts from some of the greatest minds in history were brought together offering views on a variety of important subjects, reincarnation being one of them.

Although mainstream Islam does not promote the concept of reincarnation, the mystical Islamic order known as Sufism does. It is also believed, by some, that this is the time and source from where Judaic Kabbalism originated, not as claimed by some, who believe it to be a rediscovery from lost work of 2nd century Kabbalists. Both Sufis and Judaic Kabbalists were tapping into older writings which revealed some of the greatest secrets handed down from all ages.

One of the best known Jewish Kabbalists born in Jerusalem during the 16th century was Rabbi Isaac Luria (1534 - 1572), also known as 'Holy Ali'. He was the mastermind behind Lurianic Kabbalah which became the foundation for perverted Judaic sects promoting sinful behaviour and nihilism by both Sabbatai Zevi (the Jewish Messiah 1666) and Jacob Frank (a self proclaimed reincarnation of Sabbatai Zevi). This topic is covered in detail in my previous book *The Left Hand Path*.

"Every Jew must fulfil 613 mitzvot (commandments from God), and if he doesn't succeed in one lifetime, he comes back again and again until he finishes." - Rabbi Isaac Luria

According to Jewish Kabbalists there is the real eternal you and there is the physical momentary expression of the ego, the self, this is essentially what we call the soul. Our conscious behaviour is a reflection of various levels of subconscious forces, layers of interlocking energy expressing and experiencing itself from various perspectives. The Hebrew word for reincarnation is GILGUL which means cycle or wheel. One of the fundamental kabbalistic texts for Jewish mysticism is the Zoha, a book which includes commentary on mystical aspects of the Torah. The Zoha talks about two types of souls.

● Unblemished souls, which come down here to fulfil their life's mission, untarnished and without sin.

● Soul which goes through the wear and tear of every day life, making their fair share of mistakes while becoming blemished along the way. According to the kabbalists, this is all part of a natural cyclical mechanism to evolve our overall consciousness.

Our immediate souls are believed to be part of a process which began a very long time ago, a process in which the collective consciousness of humanity is trying to evolve through infinite experiences within all realms and levels of that consciousness. And in concurrence with Rabbi Isaac Luria, if the soul fails to fulfil its designated purpose in one incarnation, it returns again and again until it does. Each soul descends from the higher realms of spiritual consciousness to a narrowed dense perspective of unique awareness in which the experience appears detached and isolated from all other souls and perspectives. Our ego or soul awareness transcends the purity of the spirit realm in order to experience and fulfil, even the most minor but unique experiences. No one's life is any more important, to the overall mission, than any other, as we all play our part within each incarnation, like various sized cogs in a great universal clock of growing consciousness.

According to the Zoha, the soul has five levels of separation as it transcends from pure spirit into the physical soul ego.

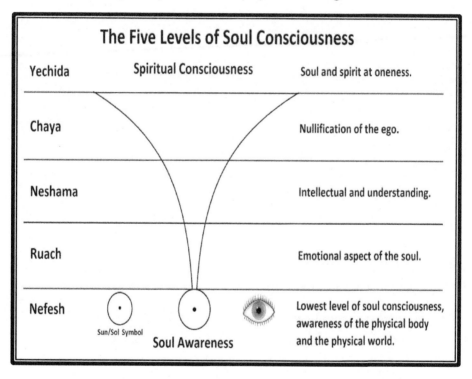

It is believed that Divine providence provides each soul with the opportunities necessary to advance through experience. However, although these opportunities are presented, at a physical level, it is ultimately up to the individual whether or not to participate. Most of us have experienced the deja vu feeling, a French term which means 'already seen'. Together with serendipity these types of occurrences are all part of our soul's connection to spiritual consciousness, interwoven within the fabric of time, space and other soul's as they advance along their similar, yet unique, paths.

Christianity, on the whole, does not believe in the concept of reincarnation. Through biblical scripture, they are led to believe that we only have one life here on Earth, after which eternal judgement takes place with a verdict based on whether we accepted Jesus as our saviour or not. Those who rejected Christ go to a place of eternal torment while those who declared Jesus to be their saviour spend eternity in paradise in the presence of God.

"And the dust returns to the ground it came from, and the spirit returns to God who gave it." - Ecclesiastes 12:7 (NIV)

"Just as people are destined to die once, and after that to face judgement." - Hebrews 9 : 27 (NIV)

"As a cloud vanishes and is gone, so one who goes down to the grave does not return. He will never come to his house again; his place will know him no more." - Job 7 : 9-10 (NIV)

Many Christian scholars and theologians are of the opinion that the concept of reincarnation was slowly removed from the official writings of Christianity due to its contradiction towards the doctrine of corporeal resurrection which ultimately undermined the need for Christ's redemptive sacrifices.

"It is believed that in 553 A.D. during the Second Council of Constantinople the idea of reincarnation was found to have no place in the Christian Church. Although reincarnation was not officially rejected at this council, those early Church Fathers who were accused of teaching the idea of reincarnation had their works banned. 553 A.D. did mark the end of the debate on reincarnation within the Christian community." - Elizabeth Jenson, *The Argument over Reincarnation in Early Christianity.*[1]

"Reincarnation has not always been so unacceptable to Church doctrine. In the early Church, as doctrinal matters were being

formulated, there was a vigorous debate about the pre-existence of souls and transmigration of souls (reincarnation). Some of the early Church Fathers, such as Clement of Alexandria (AD 150-215), Justin Martyr (AD 100-165), St. Gregory of Nyssa (AD 330-395), Arnobius (d. circa 330), and St. Jerome (AD 342-420) considered reincarnationist thinking and did believe in the pre-existence of souls. Reincarnation was a common Greek belief at the time and was discussed as a Christian possibility, especially by those with some knowledge of Greek philosophy, but it was not adopted officially. Even St. Augustine of Hippo, in his Confessions, entertained the possibility of reincarnation." - *CHRISTIAN REINCARNATION?* by Revd Donald MacGregor[2]

Even Julius Caesar and Alexander Cornelius Polyhistor made references to reincarnation being a core doctrine of the druids in Britain, Gaul and Ireland.

"The principal point of their doctrine is that the soul does not die and that after death it passes from one body into another... the main object of all education is, in their opinion, to imbue their scholars with a firm belief in the indestructibility of the human soul, which, according to their belief, merely passes at death from one tenement to another; for by such doctrine alone, they say, which robs death of all its terrors, can the highest form of human courage be developed." - Julius Caesar

"The Pythagorean doctrine prevails among the Gauls' teaching that the souls of men are immortal, and that after a fixed number of years they will enter into another body." - Alexander Cornelius Polyhistor

Muslims, on the whole, also reject the idea of reincarnation. They believe that after death their soul is escorted, by the angel of death (Azra'il), to a place where they await judgement known as Barzakh, here God sends two angels to question the waiting soul.

"To Him is your return all together. Allah's promise is always true. Indeed, He originates the creation then resurrects it so that He may

justly reward those who believe and do good. But those who disbelieve will have a boiling drink and a painful punishment for their disbelief." - Yunus 10:4 Quran

The modern main stream view of human life is one with no purpose, no evolution of consciousness and no divine spark. They consider humanity to be an accident of nature, one of cells, blood and bone, which is born, lives and dies devoid of purpose or reason. An accident, with only limited time to satisfy its immediate carnal desires and selfish wants. In my experience, this view of the evolution of man is one shared by only a small minority, If pressed on the issue most people intuitively have a sense of purpose with some form of existential connection with a benevolent source. The atheist's view of how the world came into being is devoid of any meaning, purpose or spiritual connection, making it a very lonely and empty place.

Atheist's view on the creation of the universe

The belief that there was once nothing, and for a long time nothing happened to that nothing. However, one day, for absolutely no reason, the nothing magically exploded, creating everything, and this bunch of everything, for no reason what so ever, magically rearranged itself into self replicating bits which eventually turned into dinosaurs.

Author unknown

Dalai Lama

The Dalai Lama is a title given by the people of Tibet to their spiritual leader of Tibetan Buddhism. Founded by Je Tsongkhapa (1357 - 1419), this philosophical form of Buddhism is known as the 'Yellow Hat Sect'. The Dalai Lama is considered to be a reincarnate custodian of this lineage of Tulku teachers. The current Dalai Lama, Tenzin Gyatso, was selected as the reincarnation of the 13th Dalai Lama back in 1937 when he was only two years old. On the death of the 13th Dalai Lama a search party was sent out to find his successor, the reincarnation of his soul. A handful of candidates were presented which had to go through various processes to ensure their connection and validity to the previous leader. One test consisted of showing the boy pairs of objects, one which belonged to the last Dalai Lama and the other of no importance. In every case Tenzin Gyatso chose the correct object.

Tenzin Gyatso, 14th Dalai Lama

"Some particulars of the signs by which the authenticity of the reincarnation was attested, as reported from Tibet, are transmitted by the Delhi correspondent of The Times in the issue of October 29. Not only had the existence of the reincarnated Dalai Lama and his whereabouts been indicated in a vision, according to precedent, but also when visited by the search party, disguised as traders, he recognized their holy calling and distinguished between the status of the individuals who composed the party. He took hold of the rosary which had belonged to the late Dalai Lama, telling the beads and repeating the Buddhist formula "Om Mane Padme Hum". In a further test, when the Dalai Lama's rosary, small drum and walking stick were offered him, he chose those which had been his own in his previous incarnation in preference to the replicas presented to him at the same time—a test in which another aspirant to the office failed."
- Reincarnation of a Dalai Lama, published 1939[3]

Past life memories

This is a phenomena in which a person appears to have recollections of past lives, memories of places, people and events enter their conscious thoughts in a vivid and lucid fashion. Main stream science regard these memories as imagination or the mind just creating what they refer to as false memories. This experience has greater prevalence in children under the age of 7, possibly due to the way their minds work, as they are still under development with both hemispheres working in unison, unlike the mature mind of those over that age who's brain hemispheres have separated to work independently of one another. The soul/ego of the young child is still developing, as it transcends from higher levels of awareness towards the singularity and unique perspective of the adult's soul consciousness. Consequently, the child's mind, working as one during development, is closer to its spiritual roots than the mind of the adult. This is thought to allow the easy flow of consciousness, between his right hemisphere, which is concerned with emotion and imagination and the left side, which is more analytical, rational and logical. As a result, flashes of awareness are thought to occasionally penetrate, giving the child visions from the spiritual collective, existing beyond time and space, offering snippets of energy vibrations concerning various past lives. As the child matures, with both hemispheres working independently, his soul awareness develops to a point at which he can focus clearly on tasks relating to this realm alone, detaching his spiritual ties to consciousness as he explores his new life from a unique perspective.

It is thought, by some who believe in reincarnation, that we choose the circumstances regarding our latest incarnation. We choose our parents, our place of birth and the timing in which it occurs in order to increase the potential of fulfilling our latest objectives towards soul growth and conscious development. Furthermore, any relevant data from the spirit realm and previous lives, deemed necessary for the fulfilment of future objectives is presumed to be allowed to pass into the new soul in order to prime it for future success. Some of this data is thought to manifest as past life memories or even paranormal abilities.

The case of James Leininger

James was born to Bruce and Andrea Leininger on the 10th April 1998, in the San Francisco Bay area, on the west coast of the United States. When James was 22 months old, his father Bruce took him to the city's flight museum. While there, Bruce noticed that James, although very young, appeared to have an unusual fascination with aircraft from the Second Word War. Perplexed by this, Bruce and James spent almost three hours looking at the museum's exhibits. During the months which followed, James began to suffer from traumatic nightmares in which he would often lay on his back kicking his legs in the air while crying out to his mother "air plane crash, on fire, little man can't get out". At this time James had not been subjected to any form of media influence which could have promoted these types of thoughts in his fragile mind, only the visit to the museum, which did not display such vivid material. These nightmares increased in occurrence to 3-4 times per week, along with his apparent obsession with toy planes and air craft carriers. Alarmed by all this, Bruce and Andrea set about trying to get to the bottom of their son's strange behaviour. As James' speech improved he was able to relate his visions to his parents in more detail. They discovered that the best time for this was moments before James went to sleep, a time when he appeared semi conscious and drowsy. Throughout this period James frequently talked about the life of a World War Two fighter pilot, who had been shot down and killed. One evening, as Bruce noticed his son getting drowsy, he began to ask James some delving questions.

Bruce **"What happened to your plane?"**

James **"It crashed on fire."**

Bruce **"Why did your airplane crash?"**

James **"It got shot."**

Bruce **"Who shot the plane?"**

James **"The Japanese."**

Bruce **"What kind of plane did you fly?"**

James **"A Corsair."**

At this point James' father, who was initially sceptical about reincarnation, began to take his son's stories seriously, and over the following months began deeper preliminary research into the matter. At one point while Bruce was flicking through a book on WW2 planes, James came over, pointing to one of the pictures and said **"That is a Corsair, and they get flat tyres all the time."**

Bruce **"Do you remember where your plane took off?"**

James **"Took off from a boat."**

Bruce **"What was the name of the boat?"**

James **"Natoma."**

Bruce **"That sounds Japanese."**

James **"No, it was American."**

Bruce **"Do you remember what your name was?"**

James **"James."**

Bruce **"Do you remember any friends?"**

James **"Jack Larson."**

After more research Bruce discovered that there had indeed been an aircraft carrier during World War Two named *Natoma Bay*. Not only that, there was also a pilot, who served on the ship, by the name of Jack Larson, who happened to still be alive and living in Arkansas.

Many of James' drawings and artwork during this period would be signed by him as 'James 3'.

Bruce **"Why do you sign your name as James 3?"**

James **"Because I'm the 3rd James".**

One afternoon Bruce was flicking through a book about the battle of Iwa Jima, which he had bought, as a gift, for his own father's birthday. While turning the pages, James came over pointing at an aerial photo of the island and said "That was where my plane was shot down".

After more research, Bruce eventually found out that one American pilot, from the *Natoma Bay*, was shot down during an attack on Iwa Jima, and to his astonishment the pilot's name was James Huston Junior.

James would describe being shot down by a direct hit to his engine, which sent him crashing on fire into the sea. On further investigation, it came to light that another pilot, a rear gunner by the name of Ralph Clarbour, who was also still alive, flew from the *Natoma Bay* during that mission and distinctly remembered being next to James Huston's plane when it was hit by anti aircraft fire.

"I would say he was hit head on, right in the middle of the engine," - Ralph Clarbour

Sceptics to this apparent occurrence of reincarnation are still not satisfied, regarding James as an elaborate story teller, who's imagination just got lucky with various names he may have overheard in conversations. However, coincidences of this magnitude, appear to many, as paranormal evidence of some form of soul connection or reincarnation. Although James Hudson did not die in a Corsair, he was one of a handful of pilots who flew them. Sceptics point out that James, the boy, could have remembered the name of the aircraft from his visit to the museum at 22 months old. However, after further investigation, it was discovered that the air museum did not have a Corsair on display at the time of the Leininger's visit. It only appeared in the museum a few years later. Dr Jim Tucker MD, a professor of psychology and neurobehavioural studies at the University of Virginia, suggests that the description of James' behaviour as a young boy, concerning his apparent memories of James Hudson life, display elements of post traumatic trauma; and that, as a child, he was reliving and expressing James Hudson's final moments in his day to day activities. This is similar to other children who had been traumatised in this life and displayed, what he called post traumatic play.[4]

Reincarnation, James Leininger & James Hudson Junior

James Leininger	James Hudson Junior
· Signed drawings as James 3	· Was James Junior
· Flew off the Natoma	· Pilot on the USS Natoma Bay
· Flew a corsair	· Had flown a corsair
· Shot down by the Japanese	· Shot down by the Japanese
· Died at Iwa Jima	· The only pilot killed during the Iwa Jima operation
· Airplane shot in the engine, crashed in the water, that's how I died.	· Eye witness report said Hudson's plane shot in the middle of the engine.
· Nightmares of plane crashing and sinking in the water.	· Plane crashed into the water and quickly sank.
· Jack Larson was there.	· Jack Larson was pilot of plane next to Hudson.

In some cases concerning past life memories, the individual may develop phobias relating to trauma experienced in a past life. For example, a person with a fear of water could have drowned in a previous incarnation, and someone with a fear of knives could have had a lethal experience in relation to knives in a prior life. Professor Ian Stevenson, head of psychiatry at the University of Virginia during the late 50s and 60s, undertook extensive research into the field of reincarnation and past life memories especially in children. In his book 'Reincarnation and Biology' he outlines 225 cases in which people from all over the world had memories of previous lives. He also makes a link between bodily defects, birth marks and disabilities which people were born with in relation to memories of past lives. For example : a Burmese girl, born with her lower right leg missing, talked about another life where she was run over by a train, and a Turkish boy who's face was congenitally underdeveloped on the right side, would talk about the life of a man who died from a shot gun wound to the face.[5]

Is it the case, that while enough necessary data from a previous life is allowed to seep through into the new foetus, emotional baggage attached to memories permeating from higher realms of spiritual consciousness could manifest within the new soul in a physical manner? This could very well be a possibility, as the subconscious is very much in tune with our emotional aspects of memory. Furthermore, during the early stages of a child's development, when its brain hemispheres are still working in unison, emotion and right brain stimuli play a leading role in those formative years. Consequently, after the child's brain hemispheres have developed to a point at which they separate, around the age of 7, their soul awareness matures to a point at which it overrides and dominates any residual spiritual interference. It is well documented that children who experience these emotional loose ends concerning past lives grow out of them by the age of 7. The other explanation for this phenomena can be viewed as an underdeveloped soul, still in the process of transcending the higher realms of consciousness towards its unique point of soul awareness. Initially beginning its journey from spiritual consciousness, a place outside lineal time constraints, where a sea of consciousness acts as a collective uniting all soul experiences within a union of energy. Therefore, it is plausible to assume that, a new born child, with an immature and developing soul, still possess some form of connection to their spiritual origins. A realm in which all soul memories exist within a form of Akashic record, and that the undeveloped soul occasionally draws its influence from the spiritual realm.

Akashic Record : **In theosophy and anthroposophy, the Akashic records is a compendium of all universal events, thoughts, words, emotions, and intent ever to have occurred in the past, present, or future in terms of all entities and life forms, not just human**. - Wikipedia (Akashic Records)

Dr Stevenson concluded that, although many people have the potential to tap into memories of previous lives, circumstances and chaos regarding everyday life appear to cloud the opportunity from coming forth. Only when something of significant relevance takes place in the current life to stimulate the memory does a recollection occur. Although most Indians believe in reincarnation only 1 in 500 children experience vivid recollections of previous lives. Stevenson also suggested that the greater the emotional imprint left by a previous life, possibly due to a traumatic death, the more chance that residual energy would be picked up and recognised by a new soul. This seemed to be the case, as most of the children, who he had interviewed, with past life memories, claimed that their previous lives ended violently. He also noted that many of these experiences related to people who had lived within the same country, even the same city, and did not, on the whole, take place immediately after the previous life had expired, sometimes leaving many decades between the two.[6]

The case of Titu Singh

In 1983 a boy was born 13km outside the Indian city of Agra and given the name Titu Singh by his parents. At the age of two and a half the boy began to talk about a previous life of a man who owned a radio shop in Agra, married to a woman named Uma, who he'd had two children with. His stories grew more frequent, along with his desire to return to, what he referred to as, his previous life. He told his new parents that his name was Suresh Verma, who, on his return home one evening, was shot in the head and killed by two men. At first his mother and father dismissed his claims as pure fantasy, however, as his story became persistent and more detailed, his parents began to suspect there could be an element of truth in it. They asked their eldest son, Titu's brother, to look for the radio shop mentioned by Titu on his next visit to the big city, this he did a few days later. To his surprise, there was a radio shop with the name Suresh above it and after making enquiries within, he discovered that it was now owned by a widow called Uma, who had taken over the shop and the care of her two children after the shooting and murder of her husband a few years prior. After a brief but intense conversation Uma went off to tell her mother and father in law, Suresh's parents. Intrigued by the claims made by the boy Titu, they all decided to drive out to Baad village the following morning. Once there they met the Singh family, who introduced them to Titu. He sat next to his old wife and asked "do you recognise me?" "no" Uma said. He then asked about the two children and whether she remembered a family outing to a fair in a neighbouring city, where he had bought her a selection of sweets. At this point Uma was stunned into silence. After this initial meeting together with a follow up visit to the radio shop, Suresh's family became convinced that Titu was indeed the reincarnation of Suresh Verma. When Uma took Titu to meet Suresh's two children, she cleverly mixed them in a crowd of local children to see if Titu would spot them. This turned out not to be a difficult task as Titu spotted both of them immediately. Regarding Suresh's murder, Titu even knew the names of those involved. He said two men ran up to the car as it reached the house gates, one of the men, a business man named Sedick Johaadien, fired a shot which struck Suresh in the right temple, killing him instantly. Coincidently, there just happens to be a birth mark on Titu's head, which is the same size as a bullet and in the same spot, on the right temple, where he was hit.[7]

Although many people believe in reincarnation the vast majority are confused when it comes to trying to visualise this process. In essence, truth together with nature has a poetical simplicity about it. Occam's razor is often used as a way to determine the truth from a range of options, by favouring the simplest explanation. The idea for this principle, is attributed to an English Franciscan friar named William of Ockham (c. 1287–1347), a scholastic philosopher and theologian who used a preference for simplicity to uphold the idea of divine miracles. In my opinion, some scholars and theologians, tackling this subject, over complicate the issue by creating unnecessary explanations for the situations and scenarios they try to explain. To keep the whole concept of reincarnation simple, a solid understanding of the difference between spirit and soul consciousness is necessary. From this position the apparent mystery regarding this matter becomes less confusing. Essentially, each new incarnation is just a fresh point of attention, as consciousness devolves down into denser matter focused towards an independent and unique perspective within this physical realm. The devolution of the soul from the spirit is a process, one in which some sensitive children, who's souls have not fully matured, experience vivid and lucid connections to the spirit. In most cases, this connection weakens as the child matures allowing them to experience this reality from a fresh new independent perspective. Many scholars of reincarnation suggest that the soul is constantly evolving through endless experiences, and the more diverse those experiences the faster and greater that soul growth.

Past life regression

As children age their soul awareness develops to a point at which emotional and spiritual residue concerning paranormal reflections of previous lives tends to fade. This is partly due to the separation of brain hemispheres leading to a mature detachment with spiritual consciousness, allowing the unique and independent soul perspective to fulfil its life's objectives. However, these memories never entirely disappear, it is only because the soul awareness develops to a point at which it dominates the perception of living consciousness, becoming preoccupied with its connection to the five senses, that we, as adults, rarely tune into spiritual memories. This loss of recall is not irreversible and can be stimulated at any future time. Various techniques can be offered, to an individual, allowing them to transcend their soul perspective, in an attempt, to open up the potential locked deep within the subconscious. From this adjusted point of attention, some people are able to regress, backwards in time, revealing vivid details of past lives with an abundance of memories and emotions, going back throughout history.

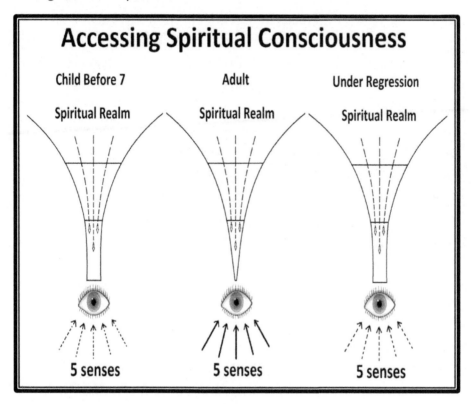

In the summer of 1980, Dr Brian Weiss the head of psychiatry at Mount Sinai Medical Centre, Miami, came across a new patient suffering from panic attacks, fears and anxiety issues. This was not uncommon for Dr Weiss, who had treated many patients in the past with similar complaints. At that time, Weiss was a disciplined traditionalist who predominantly adhered to well established scientific methods. Although studies in parapsychology were being conducted in major universities throughout the country, Dr Weiss considered such work as fringe even far-fetched. However, this was all about to change.

Catherine, the patient in question, was a 21 year old laboratory technician at the University of Miami School of Medicine. Prior to visiting Dr Weiss she was plagued by nightmares, visions of being trapped in a dark room, as she fell over things, unable to get out. Another dream saw her on a collapsing bridge which gave way sending her into the water below. These bad dreams were fuelling her panic and anxiety attacks, to a point where her work colleagues began to notice. This ultimately led to her being referred to Dr Brian Weiss for psychiatric help. For the first 18 months, Dr Weiss used traditional methods of psychiatry, in which he would, through discussion, consciously take Catherine back to her childhood, in an effort to uncover any emotional scars which might be triggering her fears. This was standard psychiatry, a technique used to re-evaluate traumatic early memories which could be defused through discussion from a new adult perspective of understanding, reason and forgiveness. This process was fairly good at neutralising past emotional baggage from influencing a patient's future well being. As the months progressed, Dr Weiss became steadily more concerned that Catherine's childhood memories were scarce and lacking in detail; All that could be established was that her father drank a lot and was abusive and her mother suffered from bouts of depression. As Dr Weiss could not pinpoint any significant event in her past in relation to the root of her fears, her symptoms did not improve. Consequently, Dr Weiss suggested that they try hypnosis in an attempt to bring forth Catherine's childhood memories in more detail. Reluctant at first, Catherine eventually agreed. On their first attempt at hypnosis Dr Weiss was able to relax Catherine enough to open up her subconscious to reveal more detailed memories. In this state, she could recall a number of traumatic experiences. She now remembered a distressing time at the dentist along with being pushed off a diving board into a swimming pool, where she became disorientated, gagged and swallowed water. Then she remembered, at the age of 3, waking up in a dark room only to notice her father standing close by, she recalled that he wreaked of alcohol and began to touch her, even down below. At this point she became terrified and began to cry, only to be silenced by his big rough hands which almost suffocated her. Back in the office Catherine began to sob, as she was now aware of part of the puzzle which had emotionally hampered her for years. Satisfied by this new information, Dr Weiss was optimistic that her symptoms would now begin to improve. However, the following weeks would prove him wrong.

For six years Catherine had been involved in a relationship with a physician named Stuart, a married man with two children. Although she had a fear of flying, Stuart, in the spring of 1982, asked her to accompany him on a medical conference trip to Chicago. While they were there, Catherine pressured Stuart into visiting the Museum of Ancient Egyptian Artefacts, a subject which had always fascinated Catherine. While being shown around the museum Catherine found herself correcting the guide who was describing a particular object. This was very much out of character for Catherine, who had not even lightly studied Egyptian history. Her correction, in this case, turned out to be correct.

On Catherine's next scheduled psychiatric visit, Dr Weiss, was expecting to see some improvement, in light of the encouraging previous meeting. Unfortunately, this turned out not to be the case, leaving Dr Weiss perplexed. He could not understand what was wrong. Suspecting that there must have be some other traumatic event which took place before she was three, Weiss decided to regress her even further back.

Although Weiss took Catherine back to the age of two she could not recall any significant memories. He therefore told her to go back to a time from which her symptoms arose. What came next took him totally by surprise.

"I see white steps leading up to a building, a big white building with pillars, open in front. There are no doorways. I'm wearing a long dress, a sack made of rough material. My hair is braided, long blond hair." [...] "My name is Aronda. I am eighteen. I see a marketplace in front of the building. There are baskets. You carry the baskets on your shoulders. We live in a valley. There is no water. The year is 1863 B.C." - Dr B Weiss *Many Lives Many Masters* P27[8]

Astonished by what he was hearing, Dr Weiss tried to focus on the task at hand. Although Catherine was recalling, what appeared to be memories of previous lives, Weiss was interested in pinpointing traumatic events which were triggering her symptoms today. He asked her to go to a time in that life where her trauma began.

"There are big waves knocking down trees. There's no place to run. It's cold; the water is cold. I have to save my baby, but I cannot. just have to hold her tight. I drown; the water chokes me. I can't breathe, can't swallow, salty water. My baby is torn out of my arms." [...] "I see clouds. My baby is with me. And others from my village. I see my brother." - *Many Lives Many Masters* P28[8]

When the session ended, both patient and doctor were awestruck. Needing time to contemplate and absorb what had just taken place, they arranged the next meeting and left the room trying to fathom the profoundness of what they had just witnessed. Although Dr Weiss was a traditionalist when it came to the scientific method, he now had some challenging data to process along with unconventional concepts concerning reincarnation. This was now getting heavy, the idea of trauma from a previous life effecting a future life seemed too far fetched to be true, but what he had just witnessed, suggested it could be the case.

The following week Catherine bounced into Dr Weiss' office in an unusually upbeat manner, saying that most of her fears and anxieties had diminished. Intrigued by all this, Dr Weiss continued with the regressions, to ascertain if there were other traumatic episodes in other lifetimes. Over the next few months, Catherine revealed many previous lives, going all the way back to ancient Egypt and beyond. Each time a life ended the consciousness would detach from the body to a place free from earthly suffering, a place where the soul/spirit would become renewed. Catherine would describe waiting in a place of peace and light, in the company of many other spirits and souls; she called these spirits 'masters'. Here they would assess her former life and prepare her for the next one. On a number of occasions Dr Weiss was able to converse with the masters while Catherine's subconscious was viewing the period between lives.

"I am aware of a bright light. It's wonderful; you get energy from this light." While Catherine was resting between lives in peaceful silence she suddenly became energised and spoke, this time in a loud husky voice with no hesitation. **"Our task is to learn, to become God-like through knowledge. We know so little. You are here to be my teacher. I have so much to learn. By knowledge we approach God, and then we can rest. Then we come back to teach and help others."** - 'Many Lives Many Masters' P46[8]

The loud husky voice spoke again in a later session, to reveal personal information about Dr Weiss that only he could have know. Catherine was now acting as a conduit, allowing the masters to communicate directly to Dr Weiss.

"Your father is here, and your son, who is a small child. Your father says you will know him because his name is Avrom, and your daughter is named after him. Also, his death was due to his heart. Your son's heart was also important, for it was backward, like a chicken's. He made a great sacrifice for you out of his love. His soul is very advanced. His death satisfied his parents' debts. Also he

wanted to show you that medicine could only go so far, that its scope is very limited." - *'Many Lives Many Masters'* P54[8]

Astonished at what he was hearing, Dr Weiss knew that Catherine had no way of knowing his father's name and that he died of a heart attack. She also had no way of knowing that Dr Weiss had lost a son a few years prior, only 23 days old. The child's heart had a rare defect in which it had almost developed backwards.

"Who," I sputtered, "who is there ? Who tells you these things?"

"The Masters," she whispered, "the Master Spirits tell me. They tell me I have lived eighty-six times in physical state."" - *'Many Lives Many Masters'* P56[8]

Catherine went on to say that there are many dimensions, different planes and different times. Each one being a higher level of conscious awareness. The plane you experience all depends upon how far your consciousness has evolved. The masters told Catherine that some of us possess intuitive powers greater than others, powers accrued from previous times. Therefore, people are not all created equal.

Using this regression technique, Dr Weiss took Catherine back through previous lives, he was able to unravel a multitude of traumatic experiences which appeared to precipitate emotional residue in the life she was experiencing now. However, by being made aware of these issues Catherine was able to work through each traumatic memory in order to defuse its impact on her present life.

Many adherents of reincarnation believe that once the soul has fulfilled the objectives it has set itself, the death process will be initiated; a process in which the soul will begin to detach itself from the body and ascend back towards higher vibrations of spirit consciousness. As it ascends it takes that current life's valuable memories and experiences with it, adding them to the ocean of experiences gathered by every soul who ever lived. This is essentially what they call the Akashic record, a sea of evolving consciousness. A newly deceased or liberated soul is thought to go through some form of life review, a process in which the most recent life can be analysed in order to reflect on that experience and to set new goals and objectives for the next round.

"For we must all appear before the judgement seat of Christ, so that each of us may receive what is due us for the things done while in the body, whether good or bad." - 2 Corinthians 5:10 (NIV)

"But the cowardly, the unbelieving, the vile, the murderers, the sexually immoral, those who practice magic arts, the idolaters and all liars—they will be consigned to the fiery lake of burning sulphur. This is the second death." - Revelation 21 : 8 (NIV)

Genius children

"Genius is experience. Some seem to think that it is a gift or talent, but it is the fruit of long experience in many lives." - Henry Ford

The word 'genius' comes from the Latin 'genius' meaning 'guardian deity or spirit which watches over each person from birth'. A derivative of the word 'genius' is 'genie' a word meaning tutelary (guardian) spirit or related to the Arabian word 'Jinn' (spirit).

There are many cases throughout the world of children born with almost super human talents. As though these talents or level of awareness came from a previous life or connection to an alternative influence. There seems to be no other rational explanation for this phenomena. The word used to describe these children is 'prodigy'; a young person who has a natural ability to do something extremely well. The word comes from the Latin 'prodigium' which means 'portent'. This is all very interesting because 'portent' is a term used to signify that something bad is likely to happen in the future. The word 'portent' is made up of two words 'port' and 'ent'. Port side is the left hand side of a boat and ent/ant is a suffix referring to 'a person who' or 'a thing that'. In Palmistry the left hand is the subconscious hand, as all the left side of the body is predominantly controlled by the right side of the brain. Is it the case that those who initially used the term prodigy knew the esoteric meaning behind the word?

Famous prodigies throughout history

- Wolfgang Amadeus Mozart : Austrian composer (1756 - 1791).

- Enrico Fermi : Italian Physicist (1901 - 1954).

- Sor Juana dela Cruz : Mexican writer, philosopher, composer (1648 - 95).

- Pablo Picasso : Spanish painter (1881 - 1973).

- Blaise Pascal : French mathematician, physicist, inventor (1623 - 1662).

- Arthur Rimbaud : French poet (1854 - 1891).

- Clara Schumann : German pianist, composer (1819 - 1896).

- Jean-Francois Champollion : French scholar, philologist (1790 - 1832).

Wolfgang Amadeus Mozart was a composer during the classical period of the late 18th century. Born in Salzburg, Austria, Mozart showed extraordinary ability in music at a very young age. By the time he was five he had already composed a number of pieces and even performed in front of royalty. By the time of his premature death, at the young age of 35, he had composed over 600 works, many of which are considered to be musical masterpieces, the standard of which is rarely seen. When we analyse Mozart's birth/natal chart some interesting and remarkable revelations come to light.

Wolfgang Amadeus Mozart's Birth Chart

January 27th, 1756, 8am, Salzburg, Austria.

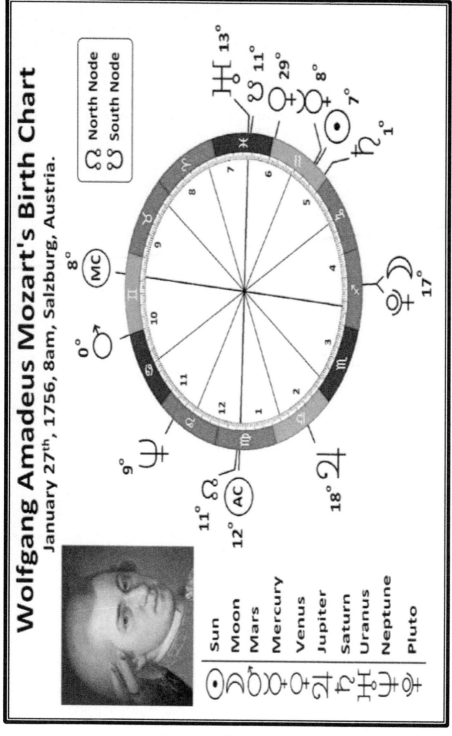

☊ North Node
☋ South Node

Sun	☉
Moon	☽
Mars	♂
Mercury	☿
Venus	♀
Jupiter	♃
Saturn	♄
Uranus	♅
Neptune	♆
Pluto	♇

Viewing the chart we see Mozart's North and South nodes are in a very interesting position. These nodes are points in space where the Moon's orbit crosses the Earth's orbit as it goes around the Sun. They represent the path of the soul as it journeys from one life into the next.

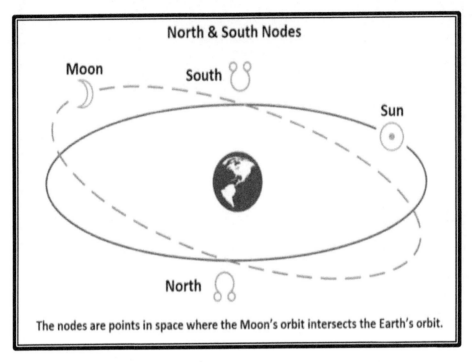

North & South Nodes

Moon

South

Sun

North

The nodes are points in space where the Moon's orbit intersects the Earth's orbit.

Since the Sun represents our focal conscious soul and the Moon represents our spiritual subconscious, the nodes express our soul's path through this life. The South Node relates to our past, our roots and where we came from, whereas the North Node gives us a clue as to what our soul purpose is, essentially what we came into this life to experience. Many of us incarnate expressing, at an early age, our South Node's chart position characteristics. However, as we grow and develop we should strive to move in the direction of the North Node, as it clearly offers us our individual path towards soul development. Mozart's South Node is opposite his Ascendant, it is the entry point on his soul's journey, a point at which he should naturally feel comfortable. The soul enters here bearing gifts or baggage from previous lives. The right side of the chart relates to relationship identity, whereas the left side is personal identity. As Mozart's soul entered in the relationship side of the chart, he would have naturally felt comfortable in the company of others, being dependent and heavily influenced by those around him as a child. However, Mozart's soul path is clearly marked by the position of his North Node which falls on his ascendant. The ascendant in a birth chart represents first impressions, the superficial you. If we view this concept as a stage, the soul/focal awareness is our expressive personality. This is the front of the stage, what others will see as we project our ego. Our subconscious, on the other hand, is everything behind the stage, including the dressing rooms, props and scenery. The AC (ascendant) itself represents first impressions, the moment we walk out onto the stage. For Mozart, this essentially became his soul's purpose, a path to which he fulfilled exceptionally well.

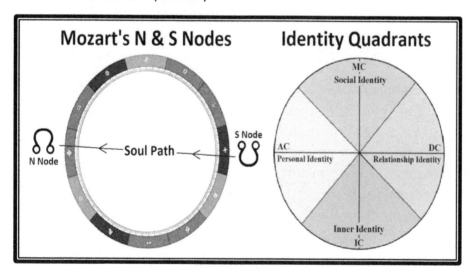

The North Node is conjunct to Mozart's Ascendant in the sign of Virgo (I examine), this is the sign of the perfectionist, it is a mutable earth sign expressing its potential in a practical way, its mutable qualities allow for flexibility, variability and change relatively quickly. For Mozart his karmic path was ultimately expressed through his personal identity and ego, allowing his talent and ability to manifest mutable changes to his music and performances, while keeping a high standard of perfection throughout.

Could it be that Mozart's relatively young passing was, in essence, due to the soul initiating the death process because it had fulfilled all of its objectives here on Earth?

Sun conjunct Mercury in the 5th house within the sign in Aquarius (I know) : This conjunction and placement reveals a great deal concerning Mozart's personality. This is the house of artistic creativity, entertainment, romance, pleasure, gambling and hobbies. The Sun represents where Mozart's focal attention lies, conjunct with Mercury, the planet of communication. This all comes together within the sign of Aquarius, a sign representing qualities of genius, independence, uniqueness and innovation. Saturn being only 6 degrees away from this conjunction offers its qualities of order, control, hard work and perseverance into the mix. Being the joint ruler over the sign of Aquarius, its restrictive and orderly energies can be viewed as a necessary ingredient for success in any developing venture.

Moon conjunct Pluto in the 4th house within the sign of Sagittarius (I seek) : The Moon represents the subconscious and emotional needs. Pluto is the planet of transformation, death and rebirth. The 4th house represents the home environment, family and sense of security. With Pluto conjunct the Moon here, in Sagittarius, the individual will have an emotional need to keep moving, dismantling their home environment for the next adventure. Sagittarius in Tarot is represented by the Chariot card, ruled by Jupiter, this is the optimistic and Jovial explorer looking for another place to go. A mutable fire sign bringing passion and flexibility to the home environment. Both Pluto and the Moon are primarily concerned with the subconscious. Pluto, being associated with Kether, the first Sefirot on the Kabbalistic tree of life, is regarded as the closest planet to Creator consciousness. Furthermore, being conjunct with the Moon should occasionally promote intense spiritual / subconscious energy, giving rise to a powerful emotional home environment for Mozart.

4th House of Home and Family

Moon

Subconscious Emotional Needs

THE CHARIOT.

'I Seek'

Pluto

Transformation, Death & Rebirth

"While Wolfgang was young, his family made several European journeys in which he and Nannerl (Mozart's sister) performed as child prodigies. These began with an exhibition in 1762 at the court of Prince elector Maximilian III of Bavaria in Munich, and at the Imperial Courts in Vienna and Prague. A long concert tour followed, spanning three and a half years, taking the family to the courts of Munich, Mannheim, Paris, London, Dover, The Hague, Amsterdam, Utrecht, Mechelen and again to Paris, and back home via Zurich, Donaueschingen, and Munich" [...] "The family trips were often challenging, and travel conditions were primitive. They had to wait for invitations and reimbursement from the nobility, and they endured long, near-fatal illnesses far from home." - Wikipedia 'Mozart'

"When I am travelling in a carriage, or walking after a good meal, or during the night when I cannot sleep; it is on such occasions that ideas flow best and most abundantly." - Mozart

Jupiter in the 2nd house within the sign of Libra (I balance) : The 2nd house represents personal finance, material possessions and concepts of value. Jupiter is the planet of abundance, optimism and expansion.

With Jupiter in this chart position Mozart has the potential to generate great wealth, expanding his personal finances and assets along the way. However, being in the sign of the balancing scales, this cannot be taken for granted, although the potential is there, a sensible balanced approach is necessary in order to hold onto that wealth.

"Mozart made a fortune during his brief lifetime but seemed determined to spend every cent of it, leading to lifelong money woes and centuries of misconceptions about his final years." […] "Records show that by the 1780s, Mozart was earning as much as 10,000 florins a year, and a letter from Mozart's father stated that he had been paid 1,000 florins for just one concert performance. At a time when labourers took home 25 florins annually." […] "The family was forced to move several times, and some historians believe Mozart may have squandered large sums of money at the gambling table, although others believe betting was just a pastime, not a compulsion." - How Mozart made and nearly lost a fortune, Biography.com[9]

Mars in the 10th house within the sign of Gemini (I think) : The 10th house represents a person's career. This is in the sign of Gemini which is associated with the hands and arms. Mars is the planet of proactive movement, energy and fiery passion. A person with this planetary placement should have a natural dexterous ability when using their hands and arms in their chosen career. Mozart was a talented man, he was proficient at the keyboard and violin from a very early age, later to become a competent conductor as well as composer. Mars in this position offers the individual ample energy to further their career path. However, as a consequence of this fiery temperament it can give rise to the possibility of conflict. Mozart began his career in Salzburg, employed by Prince Archbishop Colloredo, the ruler of Salzburg. Mozart developed animosity towards the Archbishop, accusing him of stifling his progress.

"Mozart and the archbishop (His employer) nearly came to fisticuffs in early May 1781. On May 9, 1781, Mozart wrote from Vienna to his

father, "I am still seething with rage! And you, my dearest and most beloved father, are doubtless in the same condition. My patience has been so long tried that at last it has given out. I am no longer so unfortunate as to be in Salzburg service. Today is a happy day for me." - *The day Mozart lost it with the Archbishop.*(10)

"When Wolfgang finally jumps ship from the archbishop's retinue while in Vienna in 1781, he reports that in a confrontation with Colloredo's chamberlain, he was called 'clown' and 'knave', and was tossed out of the room with a kick in the ass." [...] "I am forgetting that this was probably done by order of our worthy prince archbishop." - Bruce Lamott 'Mozart in Salzburg'(11)

Mozart's T-Square : T-Squares in a person's chart are aspects and areas denoting tension. Planets positioned at cross purposes to one another. In Mozart's chart, we see a T-Square between his Ascendant, his Moon/Pluto conjunction and Uranus opposite the AC (ascendant).

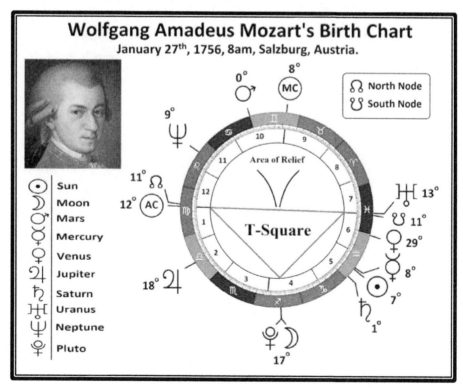

Wolfgang Amadeus Mozart's Birth Chart
January 27th, 1756, 8am, Salzburg, Austria.

Although these areas grate against one another generating pressure and stress, the point furthest away from this T-Square is regarded as a safe haven, a place where the individual finds relief. In Mozart's case the balance between his family life, his personal identity and his relationships with others acts like a pressure cooker, finding a release from the tension through his 10th house of career and 9th house of long distance travel.

"A man of ordinary talent will always be ordinary, whether he travels or not; but a man of superior talent will go to pieces if he remains forever in the same place." - Mozart

When analysing the statistics relating to Mozart's chart, the energies and characteristics of the dominant planets, signs and elements should have some impact on the man's personality and overall life.

In the following bar chart we see the planets Mercury (communication), Uranus (progressive) and Pluto (transformation) playing a leading role when influencing Mozart's life and behaviour. Mercury is the planet of communication and the thinking process; Uranus represents innovation, progressiveness, novelty and enlightenment together with a rebellious streak. Pluto is the planet of transformation, promoting the ability to throw out the old to make way for the new. This would have helped Mozart move from one project to the next very quickly. His dominant signs are Aquarius (I know), Sagittarius (I seek) and Virgo (I examine). A person with these dominant signs would be receptive to intuitive wisdom, together with a desire to seek new adventures by travelling around a great deal. The Virgo aspect would promote an analytical approach to most situations where Mozart would feel the need to examine his experiences in fine detail. Mozart's dominant houses are the 5th (creativity), 4th (home/family) and the 7th (relationships/marriage). This almost perfectly sums him up, with creativity being the main driving force behind Mozart's life.

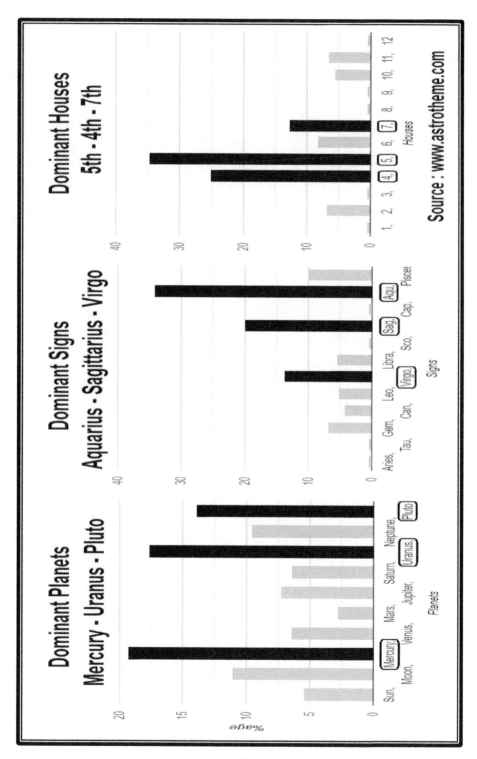

Source : www.astrotheme.com

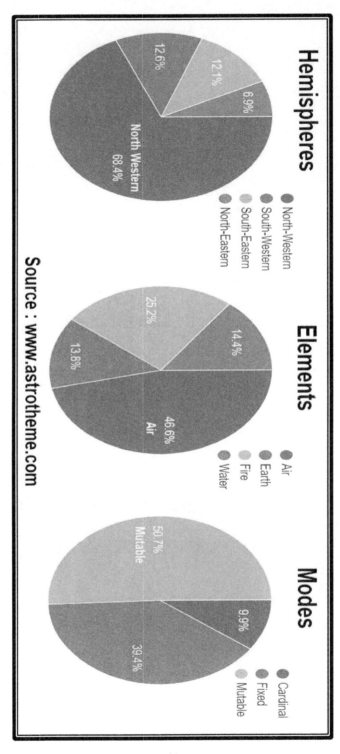

Source : www.astrotheme.com

In the above chart we see the dominant hemispheres, elements and modes for Mozart's birth chart. The north west hemisphere relates to the bottom right portion of the chart, the 4th, 5th and 6th houses. These people are generally happier within their home environment and around others, focusing their attention on being creative and enjoying home pleasures. The element which dominates Mozart's disposition is air, an element relating to the mind and the thinking process. Out of the three modes we find Mozart mostly influenced by mutable energy. This gives him a great deal of flexibility in his day to day activities. To sum up, Mozart would be content being creative at home utilising his flexible thinking ability, while enjoying the pleasures of life.

If the concept of reincarnation is a true phenomena, with various objectives to fulfil during each incarnation, some being relatively mundane by today's standards of success, then our time here as aspects of consciousness observing itself from various perspectives, should not be taken too seriously and we as individuals should enjoy the journey.

"Man suffers only because he takes seriously what the gods made for fun." - Alan Wilson Watts, *Become what You are.*

Although an astrological birth chart can give you an insight as to your soul's purpose, the sheer size and scope of the overall development of this divine project seems to be what matters. Within that project, no matter how big or small your immediate role appears to be, it still has value. The knock on effects of just a simple action or word, during one's lifetime, can have an exponential influence over future events and generations, creating ripples which redefine the course and direction of our collective development.

"You could not remove a single grain of sand from its place without thereby changing something throughout all parts of the immeasurable whole" - Johann Gottlieb Fichtein The Vocation of Man (1800)

"It used to be thought that the events that changed the world were things like big bombs, maniac politicians, huge earthquakes, or vast population movements, but it has now been realized that this is a very old-fashioned view held by people totally out of touch with modern thought. The things that change the world, according to Chaos theory, are the tiny things. A butterfly flaps its wings in the Amazonian jungle, and subsequently a storm ravages half of Europe."
- Good Omens, by Terry Pratchett and Neil Gaiman[12]

In one way the interaction between all variations of perception appears to be delicately fragile if effected by the movement of a butterfly thousands of miles away, but on the other hand, the overall development of this collective consciousness seems robust and perpetual, catering for every eventuality to play out while keeping its unfolding evolution ongoing. It seems apparent that no matter where you find yourself in life, what your status or role is, you are an essential part of the whole, and without your contribution, this impressive and elaborate interwoven physical experience could go in an entirely different direction. I would suggest that in order to advance not only your individual soul's evolution but that of the collective, it is essential that you are not afraid to follow your own intuition, as that intuition is tethered to your spiritual subconscious.

Sometimes we find our subconscious taking over in a given situation, making us do or say things which appear out of character. A single comment or action's knock on effects ultimately steer the outcome in a totally new, sometimes unwanted, direction. Although the situation seems important and unsettling to the individual at the time of the intervention, the consequence of that chain of events continuing unchallenged could have allowed the person to go down a path counter-productive to the initial goal's set by the soul. For example, while dating a person you adore, thinking they are your perfect match, one of you may say or do something out of character, the consequence of which quickly brings the budding relationship to an abrupt end. An outside influence could also come along to intervene, setting in motion a situation which ultimately drives you both apart. This may very well be the result of a subtle but effective influence from the spirit realm.

"I am confident that there truly is such a thing as living again, that the living spring from the dead, and that the souls of the dead are in existence." - Socrates, Plato, *Phaedo* 72c-82e: "On the Soul"

"I did not begin when I was born, nor when I was conceived. I have been growing, developing, through incalculable myriads of millenniums. All my previous selves have their voices, echoes, promptings in me. Oh, incalculable times again shall I be born." - Jack London, *The Star Rover*.

"Regret is worthless - don't worry, you'll get another chance to prove yourself... In This life or another."- Bert McCoy

"The soul comes from without into the human body, as into a temporary abode, and it goes out of it anew... it passes into other habitations, for the soul is immortal." - Ralph Waldo Emerson

"I could well imagine that I might have lived in former centuries and there encountered questions I was not yet able to answer; that I had to be born again because I had not fulfilled the task that was given to me." - Carl Jung

"Friends are all souls that we've known in other lives. We're drawn to each other. That's how I feel about friends. Even if I have only known them a day, it doesn't matter. I'm not going to wait till I have known them for two years, because anyway, we must have met somewhere before, you know." - George Harrison

"He saw all these forms and faces in a thousand relationships... become newly born. Each one was mortal, a passionate, painful example of all that is transitory. Yet none of them died, they only changed, were always reborn, continually had a new face: only time stood between one face and another." - Herman Hesse, Nobel Laureate

"The souls must re-enter the absolute substance whence they have emerged. But to accomplish this, they must develop all the perfections, the germ of which is planted in them; and if they have not fulfilled this condition during one life, they must commence another, a third, and so forth, until they have acquired the condition which fits them for reunion with God." - *Zohar*, one of the principal Cabalistic texts

Notes for chapter 3

Elizabeth Jenson, The Argument over Reincarnation in Early Christianity. University of UTAH. Historia: the Alpha Rho Papers.

(2) Revd Donald MacGregor, CHRISTIAN REINCARNATION? CANA Publication. Page 6.
https://www.cana.org.uk/wp-content/uploads/2013/11/Study-Book-3-Christian-Reincarnation-for-the-web.pdf

(3) Reincarnation of the Dalai Lama, 4th November 1939. Nature.
https://www.nature.com/articles/144779a0

(4) Jim B Tucker MD. The case of James Leininger: an American case of the reincarnation type. Case study. Viginia.edu. 2016.
https://at.virginia.edu/2uM3YoW

(5) Professor Ian Stevenson, Reincarnation and Biology. ISBN : 0275952827, Published by Praeger, 1997.
https://www.goodreads.com/book/show/594522.Reincarnation_and_Biology

(6) Jesse Bering, Ian Stevenson's Case for the Afterlife: Are We 'Skeptics' Really Just Cynics? Scientific America, 2013.
https://blogs.scientificamerican.com/bering-in-mind/ian-stevensone28099s-case-for-the-afterlife-are-we-e28098skepticse28099-really-just-cynics/#

(7) Trutz Hardo, 30 Most Convincing Cases of Reincarnation, p49-52, ISBN 9788184950069, 2009.
http://www.jaicobooks.com/j/PDF/30%20Most%20Convincing%20case.pdf

(8) Brian L Weiss MD, Many Lives Many Masters. 1988, Fireside publishers.
https://www.amazon.com/Many-Lives-Masters-Prominent-Psychiatrist/dp/0671657860

(9) Barbara Martinzani, How Mozart made and nearly lost a fortune. 2019, Biography.com.
https://www.biography.com/news/mozart-pauper-lost-fortune

(10) Jennifer Hambrick, The day Mozart lost it with the Archbishop, 2016, WOSU Radio.
https://radio.wosu.org/post/mozart-minute-day-mozart-lost-it-archbishop#stream/0

(11) Bruce Lamott, Mozart in Salzburg, Philharmonia Baroque Orchestra and Chorale. https://philharmonia.org/mozart-in-salzburg/

(12) Terry Pratchett and Neil Gaiman, Good Omens: The Nice and Accurate Prophecies of Agnes Nutter, Witch (Cover may vary). 2006. https://www.amazon.com/Good-Omens-Accurate-Prophecies-Nutter/dp/0060853980

Chapter 4. Meditation

There are many ways to connect with the subconscious in order to alter your point of attention and perspective of reality. Along with hypnosis, meditation is one of the best ways of accessing the great potential hidden deep within the subconscious.

Looking for consciousness in the brain is like looking inside a TV set for the actors, it cannot be measured in a traditional physical sense. The majority of people living in the modern materialistic world are preoccupied with things concerning the focal conscious mind and are fast losing the ability to take control and influence their own realities. If you are not aware and in control of the mechanisms relating to how you perceive reality then someone else will take the reins and create it for you. Your consciousness can be divided into three areas : your focal conscious awareness, which is only a small fraction of the mind; the sub-conscious, which makes up the vast majority of the overall capacity of the mind; and the higher mind or source collective. Together they form a triad of consciousness from which our perceived reality is generated.

Outside the human biological experience is energy, vibrations of all shapes and sizes. When we focus on specific frequencies, in line with our own thinking processes, those energy vibrations are picked up by our biological senses and decoded in the mind as perceived reality. Whatever belief system an individual has, will shine a spotlight on those frequencies in line with their preconceived view of the world, and like a magnet will draw towards them compatible energies, adding more validity to that initial belief system, this is sometimes referred to as a feedback loop. Harmonising thoughts will home in on harmonising frequencies, drawing them back through the five senses adding to the perception of a happy, balanced reality. Equally, disharmonious thoughts of sadness, anger, anxiety and despair will marry your inner vibrations with those outer frequencies in order to generate a perception reflecting those negative emotions. As participants of the human collective, we all contribute towards the creation of our physical reality, as transmitter/receivers of energy vibrations, we all influence each other with our thoughts and feelings. It is therefore important to choose the company you mix with. It is easy to be happy when all those around you are happy, so by helping others you are also helping yourself.

The focal consciousness of humanity shares a common collective within this physical realm of human behaviour, our souls interact on a biological level, within the limitations of time and space. Our subconscious, the dominant part of our mind, also interacts within a collective, outside the constraints of time and space, within the spirit realm. This huge capacity of consciousness interacting on a subconscious level is the engine of our perception of reality. The subconscious being 70-95% of our mind, and as a collective, is responsible for the potential offerings of energetic frequencies surrounding our physical reality. From that external potential our focal consciousness homes in on matching frequencies which harmonise with its specific disposition at any given time. This is how the feedback loop is created and how we perceive reality. Whoever controls our subconscious controls the game, they dictate the boundaries within the potential to our perceived reality through limiting the scope of the subconscious.

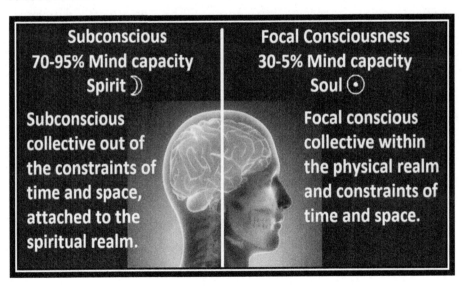

Subconscious	Focal Consciousness
70-95% Mind capacity	30-5% Mind capacity
Spirit ☽	Soul ☉
Subconscious collective out of the constraints of time and space, attached to the spiritual realm.	Focal conscious collective within the physical realm and constraints of time and space.

When a child is born, for the first two years of its life, its conscious mind is in, what is referred to as, the delta state, this is deep sleep or coma like consciousness. Between two and six the child's brain activity increases into the theta state, this is very much like being in a hypnotic trance, where the subconscious is fully open and acts like a sponge, downloading massive amounts of unfiltered information, perceptions and experiences about the world and how it works, mixing the real world with the child's imagination. This is when we are programmed, during those early years, with our own unique beliefs, a reflection of our immediate surroundings, our parents behaviour, and our interaction with the community. We are essentially programmed before our focal conscious mind has developed to a point at which it can filter new information entering the subconscious. Consequently, most people spend the rest of their lives with beliefs and habitual behavioural patterns which they had no say in or had very little control over. For the first seven years of a child's life both hemispheres of the brain are working together.[1] As they develop, specific thought processes will eventually take place in specific hemispheres, giving rise to the mature mind of the adult.

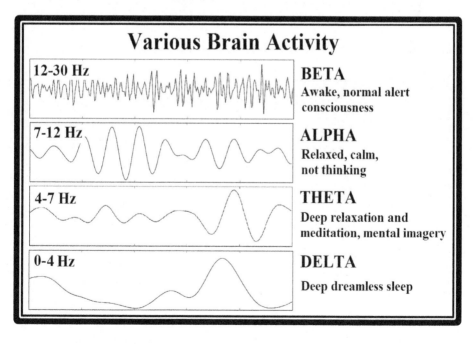

Various Brain Activity

12-30 Hz	**BETA** Awake, normal alert consciousness
7-12 Hz	**ALPHA** Relaxed, calm, not thinking
4-7 Hz	**THETA** Deep relaxation and meditation, mental imagery
0-4 Hz	**DELTA** Deep dreamless sleep

The subconscious can be compared to a computer's internal workings. At birth we come into this world with a specific karmic disposition, influenced by the orientation of universal and planetary energies. This could be viewed as the computer's Central Processing Unit, whereas all a person's habitual beliefs would be the software, downloaded in the first seven years of life. The software can be reprogrammed but the CPU is there to stay. This can go some way towards explaining why some people have easier lives than others. Each of us starts off with unique CPU karmic mapping, added to this is the software downloaded during those formative years, from then on you are on your own, master over your perception of the world, while the planetary transits continue to influence the CPU, it is up to the individual to make updates to the initial software.

The problem most people experience, as they develop, is that their focal conscious thought processes, of wants, needs and desires, don't always run in harmony with the subconscious mind's habitual beliefs and sometimes coexist in conflict. Because the subconscious is responsible for 70-95% of the mind and most of our perceived reality, the focal mind's wishes, in the physical world, are not always fulfilled. It takes a great deal of effort for the small focal mind, to manifest your desires in the physical realm, especially if it is running contrary to the massive capacity of the subconscious.

The focal conscious mind acts as a spotlight on an unlimited array of possibilities offered by the collective subconscious. Our individual subconscious is our karmic disposition together with our programmed beliefs, and because the focal conscious mind's capacity is so small compared to the subconscious, anyone wishing to influence their perception of reality, should really start by targeting the subconscious for change, as opposed to battling through their inharmonious gremlins in the physical realm, relying solely on the focal conscious mind.

Most people's minds are full of chatter, the monkey mind is a constant stream of random thoughts, images and reflections of past events and scenarios. Many of these thoughts are self-sabotaging, negative rhetoric, reinforcing Saturnian pessimism, frustrations and restrictions. This must be dealt with early and neutralised, before it grows into a reoccurring problem, which eventually has the potential to attach itself to the subconscious as a new negative habitual belief system. Through the process of regular meditation, one learns to quieten the mind, turning away from the chatter towards stillness. One major aspect of meditation is its ability to reprogram the subconscious with new positive beliefs, which run in harmony with your focal minds dreams, wishes and desires. Everything in this world is possible, not just for a few, but for all. The only thing holding most people back is their inner habitual beliefs running in conflict with their physical aspirations; yet most people in the western world have no idea how to rectify this problem, which could consequently lead them towards a better life of fulfilment, happiness and success.

Reprogramming the subconscious

Considering the majority of one's subconscious programming took place before the age of 7, in order to reprogram it, one needs to recreate the same conditions which initially opened its door during those formative years when the subconscious information downloading took place.

"Give me a child until he is seven and I will show you the man." - Aristotle

Apart from hypnosis, meditation is one of the best ways to place the mind in the theta state, it is also important to recreate thought balance between hemispheres, just like in the mind of the child, this is known as hemi-sync. One way to achieve this is to cross one's legs and arms, as the left side of the brain controls the right side of the body and vice versa, this stimulates both hemispheres. Once this is achieved and the mind has become centred, repetition and positive affirmations can be offered as mantras in order to influence and reprogram the subconscious with new beliefs running in parallel to one's new goals.

Because the subconscious is extremely powerful and is our spiritual connection to the higher mind collective; unlike the sequencing focal mind, the subconscious, has the ability to operate outside the constraints of time and space. With a new belief system in place, your perception of reality will change from within. People and events will seem coincidental, as the world around you appears to order itself towards your new objectives, illuminating those similar energies easily for the focal mind to home in on. This is how your dreams really do come true.

Meditation

Understanding the meaning of the word 'meditation' is part of the puzzle, the etymology of the word suggests it came out of 'contemplation, devout preoccupation, devotions and prayer'. Its origins come from the old French 'thought, reflection and study'. In Latin it is 'to think over, reflect and consider'. It is also derived from the root 'med', which is 'to measure'.

Meditation is constructed from 'medi', and the Latin root for medi is 'middle'. Like all other words beginning with medi, they are concerned with the middle, words like:

- Medieval (Middle Ages)
- Mediocre (a task done in a mediocre way is average)
- Medium (the medium temperature is somewhere in the middle, a spiritual medium is a person who acts as a middle connection between the physical and the spiritual realms.
- Mediterranean (the middle sea), between Europe and Africa.
- Media (reporting from the middle of a story, who are supposed to be impartial, covering from the middle ground).
- Median (the middle number in a sequence of numbers).

Words ending with "ation" denotes an action or process.

- Notation (the act of structured written communication)

- Presentation (the act of presenting a new idea or topic to an audience)
- Illumination (the act of lighting up a source)

With this in mind we can assume that the art of meditation is a physical act in which a person is trying to reach some form of middle ground, concerning the mind and its thought processes. The mind is complicated and only partially understood. In our physical world of modern science, the combined metaphysical aspect of the human mind is overlooked in favour of tangible measurable units of focal consciousness. The world of the subconscious and metaphysics, which cannot be measured by physical instruments, is conveniently dismissed as a pseudoscience. Emotions cannot be measured; the love one has for their parents or their children has no mathematical scale or equation. However, this does not mean those emotions are fictitious, on the contrary, more people's lives are ruled by feelings of love and compassion than by Pythagoras's theorem or Einstein's theory of relativity.

Many modern forms of meditation, especially western meditation are the result of fads, fashions and commercial exploitation, brought about by a new wave of interest in ancient wisdom and philosophy. One must question everything, in order to find the right path for themselves. Each one of us is different, with unique karmic mapping, varying potentials of strengths and weaknesses. Consequently, any form of religion or culture, with a one size fits all policy, is not in the interest of the individual but for the benefit of that system of control growing up around them.

"Do not make meditation a complicated affair; it is really very simple and because it is simple it is very subtle. Its subtlety will escape the mind if the mind approaches it with all kinds of fanciful and romantic ideas. Meditation, really, is a penetration into the unknown, and so the known, the memory, the experience, the knowledge which it has acquired during the day, or during a thousand days, must end. For it is only a free mind that can penetrate into the very heart of the

immeasurable. So meditation is both the penetration and the ending of the yesterday. The trouble begins when we ask how to end the yesterday. There is really no 'how.' The 'how' implies a method, a system and it is this very method and system that has conditioned the mind. Just see the truth of this. Freedom is necessary -not 'how' to be free. The 'how to be free' only enslaves you."- J Krishnamurti

"Meditation is one of the greatest arts in life, perhaps the greatest, and one cannot possibly learn it from anybody. That is the beauty of it. It has no technique and therefore no authority. When you learn about yourself, watch yourself, watch the way you walk, how you eat, what you say, the gossip, the hate, the jealousy, if you are aware of all that in yourself, without any choice, that is part of meditation. So meditation can take place when you are sitting in a bus or walking in the woods full of light and shadows, or listening to the singing of birds or looking at the face of your wife or child." - Jiddu krishnamurti

Quotes from Buddha:

- The mind is everything. What you think you become.
- It is a man's own mind, not his enemy or foe, that lures him to evil ways.
- There is nothing so disobedient as an undisciplined mind, and there is nothing so obedient as a disciplined mind.
- Nothing can harm you as much as your own thoughts unguarded.
- Peace comes from within. Do not seek it without.
- There is no path to happiness: happiness is the path.

In Buddhism the word for meditation is 'Bhavana', which means to 'make grow' or 'to develop'. Meditation helps the individual develop a different awareness, along with the energy needed to transform unwanted mental habitual patterns, trapped within the subconscious. Buddha taught many different types of meditation, each targeting specific areas requiring attention, designed to overcome various issues and to develop specific psychological states of mind. The two most common forms are:

- Mindfulness of breath (anapana sati)
- Loving kindness meditation (metta bhavana)

By sitting quietly and focusing on the in-out movement of your breathing, you can train the mind to be in the space between thoughts, during which intruding, distracting thoughts will come and go. By going back to focusing on your breathing, those unwanted thoughts should weaken and pass. With practice your ability to concentrate will improve, giving you moments of deep mental calm where inner peace will grow.

Once the mindfulness of breath technique has been mastered, loving kindness meditation can be introduced. This form of meditation can influence the subconscious with positive words and affirmations, using phrases such as:

- I am wealthy, happy and healthy
- I am peaceful and calm
- I am protected from danger, anger and hatred

Along with these positive affirmations, a good technique is to think of three people, one who you love, one who is neutral, and one who you have problems with, even dislike. In turn wish them all well, as you view them in your mind.

If this is done on a regular basis, the garden within the subconscious will begin to change, those old unwanted seeds of negative emotions like; hatred, bitterness, blame and resentment, will go un-watered, overshadowed by new seeds of positive emotions and affirmations, enabling a whole new habitual nature to grow from within.

It is my view that the whole concept of meditation is to bring one's mind and thoughts back into balance, towards the middle ground, away from extremes. If we look at the zodiac's houses, as a map of life's variety and expressions of possibility; a balanced and measured mind should be somewhere in the centre, not around the edge at an extreme point. The further away from the middle, the further the mind is away from harmony and balance, preoccupied by one specific house's characteristics. The closer your thoughts are to the middle, the more balanced the mind becomes, and the more chance of peace in the space between thoughts. The saying "to be centred" is used much in modern society, to describe someone who is mentally balanced, even without a comprehensive metaphysical understanding of what it really means.

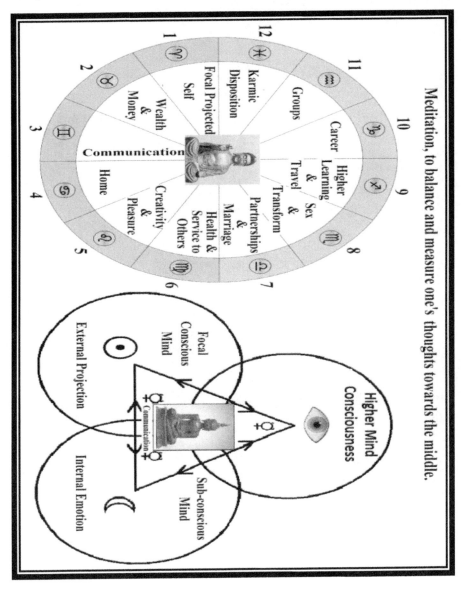

It is also a process of balancing the focal conscious mind with the sub conscious, in order to bring them in line with one another, away from conflict and disharmony. When both the focal and the subconscious are working together, the ability to influence one's own reality is greatly increased. With your thoughts you truly do make the world. This is all part of the enlightening process.

The posture for meditation is important in a number of ways. The legs are crossed to create a stable base for the spinal column to be naturally straight, one must feel comfortable in a relaxed unrestrained manner. The most popular positions are the full lotus, half lotus and the Burmese posture. The root chakra is placed firmly on the Earth, with the crown chakra positioned at the highest point. When one looks at the silhouette of the meditation position, it resembles a triangle, the three areas of consciousness. When one prays, they also create the triangle, by placing both hands together, pointing upwards. The joining of the hands is a physical expression of intention, joining or balancing both the left and right hemispheres, the focal and subconscious, in order to influence and manifest a new reality.

The power of collective meditation and prayer

"For where two or three are gathered together in my name, there am I in the midst of them." - Matthew 18:20

"You are helping us by praying for us. Then many people will give thanks because God has graciously answered so many prayers for our safety." - 2 Corinthians 1:11

Meditation and prayer work together as a mechanism to influence and alter the state of mind, which in turn will influence the state of the body and the perception of this physical reality. The habitual nature of the mind, through the subconscious, can be altered towards a balanced harmonious position together with behaviour. The state of the focal and subconscious mind acts as a spotlight on specific frequencies it is aligned to; anger begets more anger and love begets more love, it is the universal law of attraction. The familiarity of a thought will make it much easier to notice and materialise on the outside.

True meditation is to centre one's consciousness in silence, not to go anywhere, or reach for anything, just to be centred in silence. From this position of oneness, prayer and positive affirmations can be introduced for maximum effect.

"Be still and know that I am." - Psalms 46:10

"Meditate in your heart upon your bed and be still." - Psalm 4:4 (AMP)

Meditation is just sitting quietly, whereas prayer is a projection of the consciousness in an affirming way. So to create the right environment for prayer to be effective it must always begin by centring oneself through the act of meditation.

"There is nothing mind can do that cannot be better done in the mind's immobility and thought-free stillness. When mind is still, then truth gets her chance to be heard in the purity of the silence." - Sri Aurobindo

"Meditation is silence. If you realize that you really know nothing, then you will be truly meditating. Such truthfulness is the right soil for silence. Silence is meditation." - Yogaswami

Many people go to church, or their chosen place of worship, to rattle off vain repetitions of prayers which they have memorised from childhood, and are able to automatically recite unconsciously. They do this without involving any form of meditation, rendering their prayers ineffective. The whole purpose of affirmative prayer is to change our conscious perspective from within, with intent we align both the sub and focal consciousness towards a given frequency and desired goal.

When someone tries to give up smoking after 20 years, they have great difficulty persuading their subconscious, the habitual mind, to quit. Although the focal conscious mind has decided to quit, the subconscious has been offered 20 years of affirming behaviour, telling it that it loves to smoke. By centring oneself in meditation, reprogramming the subconscious becomes much easier. Prayer and positive intentions towards the new "non-smoker" can be introduced planting new seeds and a new belief system, which in turn creates a new reality.

During the summer of 1993, a controlled study was carried out in Washington DC, designed to see if a large group of 4,000 transcendental meditators could influence the city's crime rate. The meditators would, over a period of 8 weeks, use their calming influence over the cities inhabitants. Remarkably after the results were compiled, they discovered that the crime rate had indeed fallen by a staggering 23%.[2]

Quotes on meditation

"Spiritual meditation is the pathway to divinity. It is a mystic ladder which reaches from earth to heaven, from error to truth, from pain to peace." - James Allen

"Meditation is the golden key to all the mysteries of life." - Bhagwan Shree Rajneesh

"Meditation is not something that should be done in a particular position at a particular time. It is an awareness and an attitude that must persist throughout the day." - Annamalai Swami

"Meditation is the dissolution of thoughts in eternal awareness or pure consciousness without objectification, knowing without thinking, merging finitude in infinity." - Sivananda Saraswati

"If you can't meditate in a boiler room, you can't meditate." - Alan Watts

"Meditation, perhaps, is the only alchemy that can transform a beggar into an emperor." - Bhagwan Shree Rajneesh

"Meditation is not a way of making your mind quiet. It is a way of entering into the quiet that is already there—buried under the 50,000 thoughts the average person thinks every day." - Deepak Chopra

Positive affirmations and mantras

There are many ways to reprogram the subconscious, when trying to make changes as adults. Repetition is successful, but takes a while and many hours of dedication, it works by creating new automatic habits which are the domain of the subconscious. We learn our mathematical tables this way, reciting them off by heart without even having to think or engage the focal mind. To live a more fulfilled and happy life, one's internal programming must be in tune with those positive aspirations. If an individual desires a loving relationship, but has difficulty in manifesting this in their reality, it could be due to a conflicting belief system. They may, as a child, have harboured a belief of doubt and separation in the area of love, they may have difficulty not only trusting others, but also loving themselves. To rectify this a new belief must be downloaded into the subconscious, through repetition of positive mantras, one can stimulate the growth of a seed into a new belief system, while at the same time preventing any further nurturing of unwanted detrimental seeds. Once in the meditative state the person must convince the subconscious mind that he loves himself. He must repeat the mantra "I love myself", until it becomes a fixture in his habitual nature. It is very difficult to love others if one does not care much for one's self. Using this technique one can work on all areas of their lives until the subconscious is finally playing ball with the focal mind's latest aspirations. The mantra used must be simple, straight to the point and in the present tense, as though you are talking to a 6 year old child. It is no good reciting the words "I will be rich" because that is a future concept, and the future will never be in the here and now, one must say "I am rich" or " I am happy".

Positive Mantra		
I am happy	I love myself	I have lots of energy
I am wealthy	I love my life	I don't smoke
I am healthy	I love my career	I don't drink alcohol
I am slim	I love humanity	People like me

"Therefore I say unto you. What things soever ye desire, when ye pray, believe that ye receive them, and ye shall have them." - Mark 11:24 (KJV)

"Whatever your mind can conceive and believe the mind can achieve regardless of how many times you may have failed in the past." - Napoleon Hill

"As a single footstep will not make a path on the earth, so a single thought will not make a pathway in the mind. To make a deep physical path, we walk again and again. To make a deep mental path, we must think over and over the kind of thoughts we wish to dominate our lives." - Wilfred A Peterson

"Whether you think you can or think you can't, either way you are right." - Henry Ford

"Nurture your mind with great thoughts, for you will never go any higher than you think." - Benjamin Disraeli

"I attract to my life whatever I give my attention, energy and focus to, whether positive or negative." - Michael Losier

"The closer you come to knowing that you alone create the world of your experience, the more vital it becomes for you to discover just who is doing the creating." - Eric Micha'el Leventhal

"If you can believe that you can do it, the whole universe will conspire to help you." - Debasish Mridha

"If you change the way you look at things, the things you look at change." - Wayne Dyer

When trying to access the subconscious from our sequential focal conscious perspective, trapped by inherent boundaries of time and space, we come up against some difficulty. However, there are many ways to open this door, allowing us to reprogram the subconscious in order to plant new beliefs. The more of the five senses you can stimulate during the reprogramming phase, the greater the chance of success. Here are just a few ways to reprogram the subconscious mind:

- Positive affirmation: Repeating positive, present tense, statements can override negative thoughts and beliefs already lodged in the subconscious. Use simple positive phrases like 'I am happy every day'.
- Visualisation: Visualising your wants, needs and desires is a great way to stimulate the subconscious into accepting them as your new reality, conspiring with the universe to make it happen.
- Hypnosis: While extremely relaxed, with the mind in the theta state, the subconscious is open and easily reprogrammed from suggestions offered by a hypnotist.
- Subliminal audio/visual: The best time to use this method is when the mind is in the theta state, either at the start of the sleep cycle or towards the end.
- Meditation: This is one of the most popular ways to access the subconscious although it requires practice and dedication.
- Will power & habit: This is all part of repetition, with the will backing positive intent, through repetition, habits form, and from habits a new character is created.

- Auto- suggestion: Or self-suggestion is a simple way to influence the subconscious, new positive beliefs and intentions are repeatedly reinforced by the individual, until those old negative seeds and beliefs have withered away and perished.

Swimming is another great way to access and reprogram the subconscious; overlooked by many, this simple process does not get the attention it deserves. Considering water is synonymous with the spirit realm, the Moon and the subconscious, it seems a logical choice when choosing other forms of meditation and subconscious reprogramming. The action of swimming is a great opportunity to achieve moving meditation, while also stimulating many of the five senses, it really does tick all the right boxes.

- The swimming strokes are repetitive and rhythmic.
- The sensation of water flowing over the body, stimulates feeling.
- You hear the sound of the water in an isolated way.
- Helps to shut out external stimuli in a cocooning effect.
- While swimming you can focus your attention on your breathing.
- Activating hemi-sync by using both arms and legs to swim.
- Swimming can make you feel relaxed.

Once the swimmer has achieved a comfortable state of relaxation, with an easy, steady, repetitive stroke, positive mantra and visualisations can be introduced, this will open the door to the subconscious, allowing new seeds and beliefs to germinate.

Because the subconscious is a non-judgemental magnet to emotional stimuli, there is another practical way to influence it, a technique which has been known about for thousands of years. Concerned with emotions, feelings, visualisation and sensory stimuli, there is no better way to energise all these right brain triggers than the emotionally charged orgasm. Many people make the time to create a self-induced orgasm, but are they wasting a valuable opportunity to influence their reality? Instead of focusing one's attention on factory made pornographic images and all kinds of perversions, freely available on the internet; one could take the opportunity to use the orgasm as a mechanism to influence their physical wants, needs and desires, in a much boarder sense. So whatever one thinks about at the moment of orgasm, together with strong affirmative beliefs, one could sow some powerful seeds towards manifesting their own new reality. This practice may need to come under the umbrella of repetition, in order to be certain of a positive outcome, and which could alter the meaning of the phrase "coming into money".[3] One of the reasons why pornography is counter-productive to one's overall life is because it encourages the spilling of the seed while rewiring the brain with perversions and distractions. I suspect this is all part of an overall agenda, a mechanism to dis-empower many within the human population.

To live one's life by solely relying upon the focal conscious mind, in the physical realm, to guide you and solve all your problems, while ignoring the vast capacity of the subconscious; is like having one hundred radio stations, but only ever tuning into a handful. When the focal and subconscious are finally working in harmony, your life's potential is limitless, even to the point of illumination.

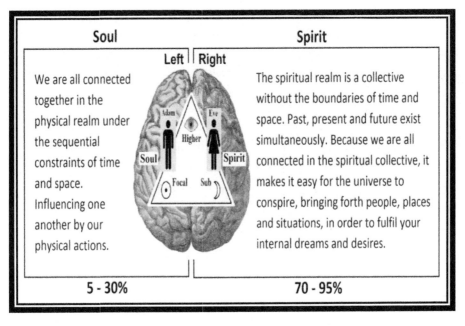

Soul	Spirit
Left │ Right	
We are all connected together in the physical realm under the sequential constraints of time and space. Influencing one another by our physical actions.	The spiritual realm is a collective without the boundaries of time and space. Past, present and future exist simultaneously. Because we are all connected in the spiritual collective, it makes it easy for the universe to conspire, bringing forth people, places and situations, in order to fulfil your internal dreams and desires.
5 - 30%	70 - 95%

A good analogy to use, when trying to understand this whole concept, is to visualise a man riding on the back of a large elephant. The man represents the focal mind, and the elephant is the subconscious. During the man's childhood, the elephant is told to go on a journey, through the forest, from A to B. This does not cause a problem during the early years of the man's life, but as he grows up and starts to think for himself, he finds his new wants, needs and desires are not in tune with the elephant, he now wants to go from A to Z. But the little man, only a fraction of the strength and size of the elephant, finds it difficult to persuade the elephant to go in this new direction; and in order to create a new path he has to fight, all alone, with the elephant and the forest simultaneously. One night the man has a dream where he is shown how to speak a new language allowing him to talk to the elephant; over the next few days the man and the elephant begin to communicate and start working together in harmony. He convinces the elephant to change course, to the new destination of A to Z. The man no longer had to struggle with the forest or the elephant, he let the enormous and powerful animal do all the hard work while he sat back and enjoyed the ride.

The elephant analogy describing the subconscious is an interesting one, because in the Hindu tradition the elephant headed God Ganesha has many similar characteristics to the human subconscious mind :

- Invokes order to remove obstacles.
- His large pot belly is said to contain the universe, past, present and future.
- He has paranormal powers.
- A snake girdles around his pot belly (snakes are nocturnal hunters, and are used to represent the subconscious).
- He has childlike innocence and behaviour, just like the subconscious, which was fully open when we were children. Consequently, when we communicate with the subconscious we have to talk to it as though it was a 6 year old child, in the present tense.

- He also represents the divine consciousness.
- The rope Ganesha holds in his left (subconscious) hand, is the weapon used to remove obstacles.
- He rides on top of a mouse or rat, which represents the human focal conscious mind.
- He symbolises life cycles which challenge us to expand our consciousness.

Once you have Ganesha, or your subconscious elephant, on the same side as your focal conscious mind's dreams, wishes and desires, anything becomes possible, even healing with your hands.

"Do not neglect the spiritual gift within you, which was bestowed on you through prophetic utterance with the laying on of hands by the presbytery." - Timothy 4:14 (NASB)

"Your inner landscape determines your outer life." - Heidi Dupree

Hand Emits Light Energy Healing with Hands   Jesus Healing   Buddha   Ganesha & Subconscious

Moon cycles and phases

The Moon is the fastest moving of all the planets and luminaries from our earthly perspective. It rotates around the Earth every 27.3 days, this is known as a sidereal month, but because the Earth is also rotating around the Sun, the orbit of the Moon in relation to the position of the Sun takes an extra 2 days, this is referred to as a synodic month, 29.5 days. Consequently, the Moon moves 12.2 degrees eastwards, occupying each zodiac house for 2.5 days. The moon produces no light of its own, only reflecting what comes towards it from the Sun, and as it moves around the Earth we experience the Moon's phases, from the new moon (conjunct with the Sun) to a fully illuminated moon (opposing the Sun).

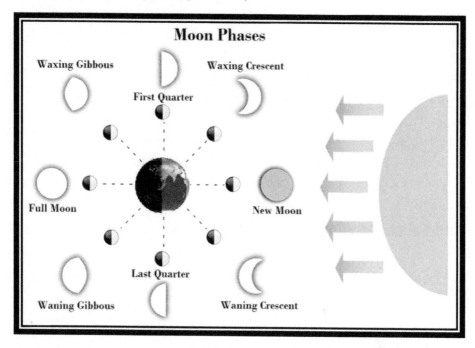

As reality is a construct within human consciousness, stimulated by our thoughts together with energies emanating from planetary bodies especially the Moon; its natural cycles and rhythms are therefore important to us when relating to all things to do with our internal subconscious and our spiritual connection to the universe. The Moon has an influence on the waters of the Earth, and on the monthly cycle of female fertility, so it is not unreasonable to expect those influences to continue throughout the waters of the body and the inner mind. With the focal consciousness being only 5 – 30% of our minds capacity, it is also reasonable to assume that the Moon's connection to our subconscious plays a role in influencing the larger elephantine part of the mind. It is also necessary to comprehend the importance of Moon cycles as they interact with the houses and signs of the zodiac.

Each month there is a new moon, which takes place in a different sign and house of the zodiac. That house should therefore become the backdrop for sowing new seeds within the subconscious and your Garden of Eden. The new moon is the start of a new cycle, it is nature's way of initiating a new beginning, or at least an opportunity to tweak that area of life associated with that house which the new moon falls in. Those 2.5 days of the new moon can be used to plant new positive seeds of intention, dreams and aspirations. It is a window of opportunity enabling us to communicate with our subconscious elephant. This is the time when meditation can achieve its greatest impact towards reprogramming the subconscious and therefore alter our perception of reality. Not only can we target those areas of life associated with the specific house the new moon falls in, but also those characteristics synonymous with the house's ruling planet, for example Jupiter would be optimism, abundance and good fortune.

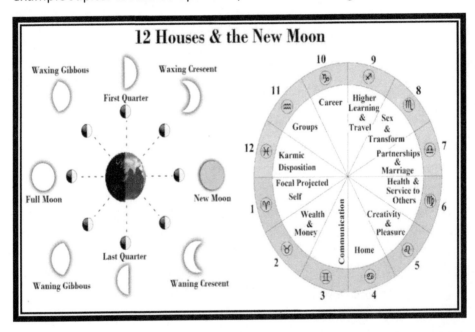

A new moon in the first house of Aries (I am), ruled by Mars (proactive energy), Cardinal fire, is the 1st house of the self, and the focal projected consciousness. During the 2.5 days of this new moon, it is a good time to initiate new beliefs about how you project yourself and come across to others, and how your ego is defined. You could take this opportunity to humble the ego or even encourage it to become more confident. This is all about you, the (I, me, mine). It is also about the head, so anything to do with the head can be brought into the picture, healing the head or whatever part of the body is associated with the house each new moon falls in.

To narrow down the zodiac house which is being activated by the new moon, specifically for you, the native's ascendant or rising sign must be taken into account in order to adjust the house position coming into play. For example, if we have a new moon in Aries, it would influence the first house for rising Arians only, and the second house for rising Taureans, the third house for rising Geminis, the fourth for Cancerians, and so on. Although the new moon's energetic influence, at source, is consistent, it will effect different areas of life depending upon which Moon sign we are born under and the position of our ascendant.

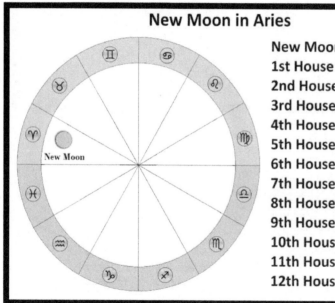

New Moon in Aries

New Moon in Aries
1st House for Aries
2nd House for Taurus
3rd House for Gemini
4th House for Cancer
5th House for Leo
6th House for Virgo
7th House for Libra
8th House for Scorpio
9th House for Sagittarius
10th House for Capricorn
11th House for Aquarius
12th House for Pisces

The full moon

While the new moon is introspective, concerning the subconscious, the full moon illuminates a particular area of life which may have been neglected by our focal attention. As the Sun is the energy source behind the focal mind, and being on the opposite side of the zodiac, opposing the bright Moon, this full illumination brings forth more of the Moon's influence, shining a subconscious light on this neglected area, pulling it back into the picture and towards the attention of the focal conscious mind.

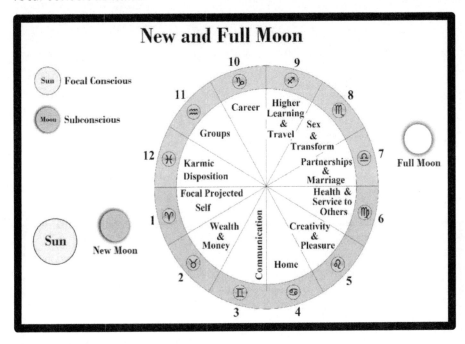

If an individual has aspirations of becoming a great communicator, to improve his communication skills; instead of placing all of his attention on the physical perspective, relying solely on that 5% of the mind, which is the focal consciousness; it may be beneficial for him to consider utilising the 95% part of the mind which is commonly dismissed. It may be advantageous to meditate during a new moon in Gemini, and for those 2.5 days of the new moon, all effort should be placed on reprogramming the subconscious, using an array of techniques designed to stimulate the elephant and the Ganesha. With this in mind unwanted obstacles can be removed in order to promote a new internal belief system and path towards better communication and thus a preferably better perception and experience of reality.

If we compare the natural cycle of the female menstrual period with that of the Moon's phases, in relation to developing subconscious reprogramming, we may get closer to understanding the natural process which may take place in order to discard old beliefs in favour of new ones.

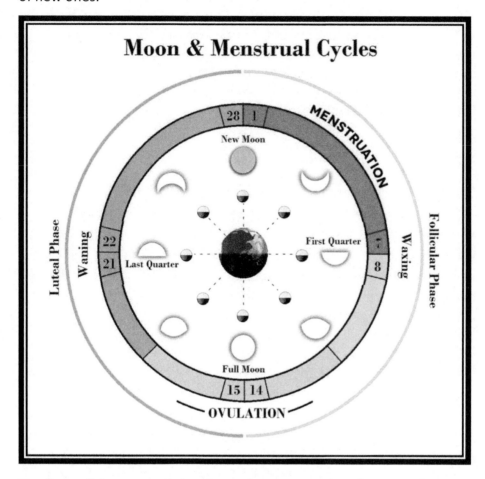

The Start of the menstrual cycle can be compared to the start of a Moon cycle, with the appearance of a new moon every 29.5 days. This can be utilised to discard unwanted subconscious beliefs from the mind. Just as the uterus discharges blood and mucosal tissue from the inner lining during the first seven days of its cycle, this time can be used to create new positive intentions, affirmations and visualisations, helping to sow new seeds and discard old ones. If one persists with regular repetitive reprogramming techniques, the new seeds should germinate. Just as a new egg is produced around 14 days, the full moon should help to bring forth those new subconscious seeds into the physical realm.

Being in tune with nature's cycles is important, modern living, with its artificial lighting, timing and electro magnetic pollution, is distorting our human biological connection to nature's rhythms, thus pulling us further away from independent self sufficiency and into the hands of the modern world of materialistic interdependency. We have moved so far away from nature's cycles that modern science cannot find any connection between lunar rhythms and the female menstrual cycle, concluding that the fact both cycles last 28 days is just a mere coincidence.[4]

Altered consciousness through meditation

"Did you know that you have the ability to go deep within your mind, beyond all five "normal" senses, to do extraordinary things you never thought possible? And that, one of these amazing abilities, is the ability to "remote view", or witness with your mind's eye: places, events, objects, and people, at any location, no matter the distance, no matter the time, whether it be past, present, or future?"
- Eco Institute 'Remote Viewing'.[5]

Remote viewing can be attempted by almost anyone and the main technique used to prepare the ground for this is meditation. To remote view successfully, the capacity and potential within the subconscious must be unlocked and utilised. Meditation puts the individual in the driving seat when it comes to steering the mind to where you want to go. Good remote viewers have developed their technique over time, centring their thoughts to a point whereby they can visualise almost anything.

In 1975 the United States Government sponsored a $20 million program called the 'Stargate Project', to determine any potential military value to psychic phenomena, including remote viewing. The program was terminated after 20 years, deemed unusable. One must ask if it was unusable, why did it take 20 years to come to this conclusion considering the amount of resources thrown at the project?[6]

On occasions police have been known to used remote viewers to aid some difficult cases. One such case took place in California in 2006. A photographer from Las Vegas named Robert Knight had become worried about his long-time friend and radio DJ, Stephen Williams. As Knight had not heard from Williams for an unusually long time. Knowing a psychic and remote viewer, Knight approached Angela Smith for assistance, finding she was more than happy to help. She gathered a team of six trainees together to see what they could come up with. After many sessions of remote viewing the team concluded, there was a body in water, a fishing net, and all this was to be found off the southern coast of California, near Catalina Island. Soon after this an unidentified body was found off Catalina Island and broadcast to the media. When Knight heard the news, suspecting it was his friend Stephen Williams, he called the county morgue and told them he may know the identity of the body. He told them Stephen had three fingers missing on his left hand, from an accident fifty years earlier. They put him on hold and went to check, and were astonished to find the fingers missing just like knight had said. After the body had been identified as Mr Stephen Williams, Knight told the police of a possible suspect. An investment adviser named Harvey Morrow, who had befriended Stephen prior to his disappearance, with the aim of investing his fortune. The police were unable to find Morrow and asked if the remote viewers could shed some light on his whereabouts. Once again, the remote viewers got together to look outside their five senses for answers. After many sessions, they concluded that Morrow had fled to the British Virgin Islands. On this tip off the police finally found and arrested Harvey Morrows. He was later convicted and is now serving life in prison for the murder of Stephen Williams.[7]

People who have perfected the art of meditation can literally detach their conscious point of attention to somewhere other than the body and its five senses. Essentially leaving their physical form to another place of their choosing. Buddhist monks are taught to master their meditative techniques as part of the training and discipline of their religious philosophy. Some senior monks have reached a point at which their detached conscious perspective has moved so far from the body that they no longer feel bodily pain from this new vantage point. This was witnessed on June 11th 1963, when Thích Quảng Đức, a Vietnamese Buddhist monk was set alight at a busy Saigon road intersection, in protest of the persecution of Buddhists by the South Vietnamese Roman Catholic government led by Ngo Dinh Diem. Thích Quảng Đức placed himself in the road and began his deep meditation technique, detaching his awareness from his physical body. At this point petrol was poured over him and set alight. Although the images are disturbing to say the least, his body never flinched throughout the whole ordeal. All that was left was his charred remains. Immediately following the event, graphic film footage and photographs, of the incident, circulated all around the world. John F Kennedy, the United States President, at the time, made a statement concerning the shocking event.

"No news picture in history has generated so much emotion around the world as that one." - John F Kennedy

Notes for Chapter 4

1) Bruce Lipton, 7 ways to reprogram your subconscious mind, How to create the honeymoon effect every day. Cheap health revolution. 2014, http://www.cheap-health-revolution.com/honeymoon-effect.html

2) John S. Hagelin, Maxwell V. Rainforth, David W. Orme-Johnson, Kenneth L. Cavanaugh, Charles N. Alexander, Susan F. Shatkin, John L. Davies, Anne O. Hughes, and Emanuel Ross, Effects of Group Practice of the Transcendental Meditation Program on Preventing Violent Crime in Washington, DC: Results of the National Demonstration Project, June-July 1993, Institute of science technology and public policy. http://istpp.org/crime_prevention/

3) Victor Daniel, Your destiny lies in the palm of your hands, About mind, body and soul. http://mindbody-soul.com/content_art_yourdestiny.html

4) Lunar Effect, wikipedia, https://en.wikipedia.org/wiki/Lunar_effect

5) Eco Institute, Remote viewing. https://eocinstitute.org/meditation/remote-viewing/

6) Stargate Project, Wikipedia.org, https://en.wikipedia.org/wiki/Stargate_Project

7) Joe Schoenmann, Seeing dead people, Las Vegas Sun, May 5 2012, http://lasvegassun.com/news/2012/may/05/seeing-dead-people-remote-viewers-nevada-help-solv/

Chapter 5. Spirit possession

Many religions and cultures throughout the world believe in spirit possession. In 1969 a global study by the National Institute of Mental Health found that 74% of the 488 groups and societies questioned believed in the concept of spirit possession. Furthermore, this belief was more prevalent among women than men. Some groups see both malevolent and benevolent spirits depending upon their culture and the spirit in question. The Egyptians thought that the spirit of a man or animal separated from its body through violent means did not move onto higher realms, instead it would linger close by the corpse. Throughout Africa many varied beliefs are held, for example, among the Gurage people of central Ethiopia there is a belief in a malevolent spirit which only effects men within their community. Once possessed, the victim experiences several degrees of symptoms beginning with loss of appetite, nausea and stomach pains. In severe cases the victim may enter a trance like stupor followed by seizures, trembling and even paralysis. If the victim does not recover naturally a spiritual healer, known as a Sagwara, is called. The first task of the healer is to establish the name of the spirit in order to begin the exorcism process. Part of this exorcism process is to administer a mixture of ensete (a flowering plant part of the banana family) native to tropical regions of Africa and Asia, combined with butter and red pepper. As the victim eats the mixture, onlookers are encouraged to chant in an attempt to persuade the spirit to leave. The ritual usually continues until the possessing spirit announces, through the Sagwara, that it is satisfied. However, this is not a permanent cure as repossessions from this type of spirit are common.

Towards the south west of Ethiopia a people known as the Sadama believe in a spirit that mostly possesses women. In almost all these cases the occupying spirit demands luxury goods in order to alleviate the onset of unwanted symptoms. However, social pressures within this culture are such that some women fake spiritual possession in an attempt to gain sympathy together with valuable gifts. These types of high maintenance spirits are also found in Kenya where many women have been accused of feigning possession, even colluding with the spirits in order to be possessed. Among the Xesibe people of South Africa, their belief in spirit possession mainly effects married women, a condition which they call 'Inwatso'. Those who develop the condition are viewed by the community as having psychic powers, with many taking up fortune telling and other divinations afterwards.

Haitian Vodou

The Haitian version of Voodoo evolved from African slaves who were used throughout the country's coffee and sugar plantations. Before the Haitian revolution of 1804, the country was a wealthy French colony known as Saint-Domingue, producing almost half of Europe's sugar and coffee imports. The predominantly west African slaves mixed their traditional African religions with the colonial religion of Catholicism, the result of which evolved into Haitian Voduo. The word Voduo means spirit and those who practice the belief are known as Vodouists 'servants of the spirit'. It is a monotheistic religion having a supreme creator God called 'Bondye' at its head which is similar to the All Mighty God of the Catholics. Bondye, being the highest principle in the universe, is so far beyond human comprehension that it is believed his will is implemented, here on Earth, through subservient spirits known as 'Iwa' or 'loa'. Bondye is also referred to as the 'good god'. However, the Vodouists do not have an evil counterpart like the Devil which many other monotheistic religions feature.

The word 'Bondye' appears to have originated from the French colonialist term 'bon dieu' meaning good god. However, after the Haitian revolution and overthrow of the French colonial government, slavery was abolished and the Catholic Church left, not to return to the country for several decades. Consequently, with limited outside influence a unique form of religion grew from within the country itself.

During religious ceremonies it is the aim of Vodouists to try and interact with the Iwa, spirits which they believe act as an intermediary between their physical world and the Bondye. Regular meetings usually take place in small temples known as 'ounfos' where they bang drums, sing and dance in an attempt to encourage the spirits to possess one of their members. When this takes place they try to communicate with that spirit in their quest for wisdom and guidance. Offerings of fruit and animal sacrifices are give to the Iwa and the spirits of the recently deceased. Once contact through possession is made, various forms of divination are used to decipher messages coming from the spirits, these come with a variety of charms, amulets and healing remedies performed within the rituals. Throughout the 20th century Haitians began to emigrate taking their religion with them and once the Catholic Church returned many Haitians embraced Catholicism while still practising their particular brand of Vodou, seeing no issue merging the two doctrines together. Today many Haitian Vodouists regard themselves as predominantly Catholic first with the famous Vodou priest and painter Andre Pierre once stating :

"To be a good practitioner of Vodou, one must first be a good Catholic." - Andre Pierre

As a result of sensationalism in movies, media and literature the practice of Vodou is largely misunderstood by most people, some even seeing it as sinister, even demonic. The fundamental ideology behind Vodou suggests that everything is spirit and that we humans, who are essentially spirit, inhabit this visible physical world, while the unseen world is populated by Iwa (spirits), all these spirits are believed to live in a mythical place called 'Ginen', a kind of cosmic Africa. Furthermore, the Iwa communicate through dreams as well as possession, interacting primarily through the subconscious.

The primary goal of the Vodouist is to 'sevi Iwa', to serve the spirits, by offering prayers and devotional rituals in return for health, protection and favours. During rituals, participants hope to be selected for spiritual possession where they often enter a trance like state as the Iwa engages with them. Each Iwa is viewed as having its own unique personality and qualities, associated with specific colours, days of the week, objects and even planets. There are over 1,000 different Iwa with varying degrees of importance, together with some Vodou priests who ultimately become Iwa after their death. They are thought to be temperamental and easily offended when offered food or items they don't like. In such cases, the possessed individual could find themselves on the receiving end of unwanted misfortune, illness or even insanity. It is interesting to note that Vodouists often talk of the Iwa residing in and around the country of Guinea, as well as being present under water in rivers, lakes and seas. Guinea is a country on the west coast of Africa, formally a French colony (1890s to 1958), where many of their ancestral slaves originated. What is remarkable is that the name 'Guinea' is very similar to the French word for 'genius', 'Genie' or the Haitian word 'Jeni' meaning the same, and as already mentioned 'genius' is thought to come from some form of attachment to the spirit realm.

With an almost endless variety of Iwa to choose from, one for each area and aspect of life; during a ceremony, the most senior spirit (Papa Legba) is saluted, he is the spirit thought to protect the home, pathways and crossroads. Following this are the sacred twins or Marasa, representing justice, truth and love. Although they are twins they also represent the number three along with mysteries associated with the veil between earth and heaven as they personify astronomic-astrological learning. This description of the Marasa has similarities to the third house of the zodiac, the twins of Gemini, which is ruled by the planet mercury, the messenger, the planet of communication between all levels of consciousness. 'Agwe' or 'Agwe-Tawoyo' is another Iwa, who could be compared to the sign of Aquarius (Acuario in French) the water bearer. This Iwa spirit is associated with aquatic life in general, being the protector over ships and fishermen while it rules the seas. 'Damballo' or 'Danbala' is a serpent spirit also associated with water. Together with his consort Ayida Wedo, they are believed to frequent rivers, springs and marshes, often depicted as two intertwining snakes. The Devil is often depicted as a serpent in many religions, the devil in Spanish, French and Greek is

Demonio, Diable and Diabolo respectively, could this be the origins of the name of Iwa Damballo? This Iwa is believed to be the first thing created by Bondye as a go-between from the spiritual creator to this earthly realm. Damballo is considered to be the sky father and the primordial creator of all physical life. This is very similar to the Gnostic concept of the demiurge, made by the spiritual creator God, at the centre of the Pleroma, created as the craftsman or artisan over the material realm.

"Damballa is seen as benevolent and patient, wise and kind, yet detached and removed from the trials and tribulations of daily, human life. His very presence brings peace, and he represents a continuum which is "at once the ancient past and the assurance of the future." As a serpent, and due to his extreme age, he does not speak, but may whistle or make a soft, hissing sound." - Iwa Damballa, Wikipedia[1]

Vodou in general teaches the existence of a soul which is divided into two parts.

- ti bònanj or ti bon ange ("little good angel") : This represents the conscious mind of the individual, focussed on the material world.

- gwo bònanje or gros bon ange ("big good angel") : This represents the subconscious, constitutes the psyche and source of our memory.

Vodouists believe that the gwo bònanje ('big good angel') can leave the head and go travelling while a person is asleep. They also believe that every individual has a predisposition which connects them to specific Iwa, they call this their 'master of the head', which contributes to their individual personality and is similar, in some ways, to the sun sign in astrology expressing a person's overt personality type. Some religious priests are said to have the 'gift of eyes' which allow them to identify the most dominant Iwa within each person. During a ceremony various drums, songs and dances will be presented designed to encourage specific spirits to come forward. Once the spiritual

121

possession takes place and Iwa identified, the 'chwal' (possessed person) is then dressed accordingly after which they will mix and interact with the congregation. These possessions can last hours or even days, leaving the host physically and mentally exhausted, often with limited recollection of the actual event.

A person who turns to the Iwa in order to inflict harm on others is known as a 'Boko'. They deal mainly with malevolent spirits because it is thought that the good spirits have rejected them due to their untrustworthy nature. These people can place curses on others which often requires a priest to overturn the curse through the help of the good Iwa.

Vodou Alter & Ceremony

Jinn and spirits in Islam

Jinn are supernatural creatures from early pre Islamic Arabia. It is an Arabic word meaning 'to hide' or 'beings that are concealed from the senses'.[2] 'Jinn' is actually pleural, with 'Jinni' being the singular. Some scholars link the word 'Jinni' to the Latin word 'genius' while other scholars try to discredit this connection. In Islam the concept of the Jinn is part of their understanding of the spiritual realm as a whole. They believe that God created various worlds, a physical realm which we inhabit together with a kind of parallel world in which the Jinn inhabit. They are said to be similar to us humans because they eat, drink and have children etc. Furthermore, from their vantage point they are able to see us, but we cannot see them. Their concept of time is very different to ours giving them extremely long lives in comparison, some being well over 1,000 years old. The Quran states that man was made from clay while the Jinn were created from the smokeless flame of fire.

"Surely We brought man into being out of dry ringing clay which was wrought from black mud, and the jinn We had created before, from smokeless, scorching fire penetrating through the skin." - Surah Al-Hijr 15 : 26-27

The Jinn are also described as beings which caused sedition and bloodshed on the earth before the creation of humanity. Although they appear to be in a realm of greater paranormal scope than ours they are thought to be below the level of angels.

"Angels were created from light, jinns were created from a smokeless flame of fire, and Adam was created from that which you have been told (i.e., sounding clay like the clay of pottery)." - Riyad as - Salihin 1846, Book 18, Hadith 39

As the Jinn were created from fire it is also thought that this influences their temperament by giving them a fiery disposition or nature. However, like humans, they too are expected to worship God and follow Islam.

"And I did not create the jinn and mankind except to worship Me." - Sahih International 51 - 56

According to some Muslim scholars many Jinn became Muslims after hearing the words written down in the Quran. Therefore, there are Muslim and non-Muslim Jinn interacting within our physical reality. The non-Muslim Jinn are regarded as part of Satan's army of malevolent devilish spirits.

"Say, O Prophet, It has been revealed to me that a group of jinn listened to the Quran, and said to their fellow jinn : "Indeed, we have heard a wondrous recitation. It guides to righteousness, and we have believed it: We will never assign divinity to anyone except our Lord."" - Quran 72 : 1-2

Just like us humans, the Jinn will also be subjected to the final reckoning on the day of judgement, eventually going either to paradise or hell. Therefore, although God gave the Jinn paranormal powers and abilities, over that of humanity, they will be held accountable if they use these powers in a malevolent way to oppress others. It is believed they can take on any physical form they wish when interacting within our earthly domain. They also have the capacity to possess the minds and bodies of other living creatures. According to one Muslim school of thought the Jinn possess people for a variety of reasons.

- As a reaction to the Jinn or their family being accidentally hurt.

- A specific Jinni becoming infatuated or even falling in love with a person.

- Malicious or wicked Jinn just doing what they like to do.

- People asking and encouraging interaction to take place.

As a consequence of this, Muslims are commanded to recite the Quran frequently and pray five times a day in order to keep malevolent Jinn away from their homes and families.

"Do not turn your houses into graves. Indeed, Satan runs away from the house in which Sūrat al-Baqarah (2nd chapter of the Quran) **is recited." -** Hadith

In the event of a spiritual possession by one of the Jinn, the Quran suggests that only by using the name of God to command the spirit to leave will it go on its way. If a name other than God is used the possibility of repossession is greatly increased.

It is also believed by many Muslims that companions of the Jinn known as Qareen are assigned, one to each person. These Qareen are thought to be responsible for revealing and passing on personal information to fortune tellers, mystics and mediums; a practice forbidden by the Quran.

"Each of them is assigned a Qareen from the jinn to command him to do evil. His name is Al-Waswaas, and he is a son of Satan who is born when a child is born to the son of Adam... The Companions said, "Even you, O Messenger of Allaah?" And the Prophet replied: "Even me, except that Allaah has helped me against him and he has submitted. Now he only tells me to do good." Mirqaat Al-Mafaateeh Sharh Mishkaat Al-Masaabeeh, 1/139

"Whoever goes to a fortune teller and asks him about something and believes him, his prayers will not be accepted for forty days." Saheeh.

"Whoever goes to a soothsayer and believes what he says has disbelieved in that which was revealed to Muhammad." Narrated by Abu Dawood.

"O children of Adam! Do not let Satan deceive you as he tempted your parents out of Paradise and caused their cover to be removed in order to expose their nakedness. Surely he and his soldiers watch you from where you cannot see them. We have made the devils allies of those who disbelieve." Dr. Mustafa Khattab, the Clear Quran

"The jinn are of three types: a types that has wings, and they fly through the air; a type that looks like snakes and dogs; and a type that stops for a rest then resumes its journey." - Shaykh al-Albaani said in al-Mishkaat (2/1206, no. 4148)

The Hadith talk about dogs and donkeys reacting to the presence of the Jinn, rousing them to bark and bray at what appears to be empty space.

"If you hear the barking of a dog or the braying of a donkey, then seek refuge with Allah, for they see that which you do not see." - Sunan Abi Dawood

The Holy Spirit (Ruh al-qudus) is mentioned four times in the Quran, consistent with the Holy Spirit mentioned in the Bible, acting as an agent of Divine action or communication. In Islam the Holy Spirit is also known as Archangel Gabriel (Jibril), the messenger to all the prophets.

In Sufism (Islamic mysticism), Ruh is regarded as a person's immortal self, their spiritual aspect of consciousness. Outside the Quran, Ruh may also refer to a spirit that roams the Earth, a form of ghost. Some Muslim commentators connect this Ruh with the faithful and trustworthy spirit 'al-ruh al-amin', who is said to have brought down the Quran to Earth and who is identified with Archangel Gabriel. These Ruh, together with the angels ascend and descend as they interact with the Creator. In Shia Islam, Ruh is described as 'a creature of God', grander than Gabriel or Michael, who was sent to inform and guide Muhammad. This Ruh is now thought to be with the Imams.

- Ruh - is the spirit or pneuma. Arwah is pleural of Ruh.

- Nafs - is the soul or ego, the psyche.

It is thought by many Muslims that the Arwah (spirits) dwell in the seventh heaven, where they eat, drink and do many things similar to what we do while being watched over by an angel called Ar-Ruh.

No one on this Earth has control over the Jinn, although some may claim they have. The three main areas in which the Jinn's world interact with ours are through fortune telling, magic and demonic possession. It is believed that various malevolent Jinn will try to entice people into some form of interaction, whether it be dialogue through a medium or suggestions entering the focal mind. Like the fisherman, they will dangle their hook, with bait attached, in this realm waiting for someone to bite. Once they have their victim they will slowly lure them into their alternative world of mischief and malevolence.

Magic has, throughout the centuries, been associated with the genie. A supernatural mythical creature found in the pre-Islamic world of Arabia. Commonly depicted as a form of spirit which lives inside lamps and bottles with the ability to grant those who liberate the genie several wishes. The term 'genie' is derived from the singular of 'jinn' which is 'jinni'.

There are many types of jinn mentioned in Islamic literature, each with different characteristics. The jinn commonly depicted as the genie in the magic lamp is considered to be a type known as a 'Marid', a word which means 'rebellious' in Arabic. These jinn are the most frequent, a powerful and classical type, often associated with water, with the ability to change their shape into whatever they wish. They are very proud with a desire to show off, often depicted with a barrelled chest and arms folded.

'Marid' Genie and the Magic Lamp

Although a person interacting with the Marid, believes they are in control, in truth, the Marid jinni is the one who controls the relationship. They may grant you, what appears to be superficial wishes, but in reality, they are luring you into a direction they want you to go, which is often contrary to your best interests. The flying carpet in Arabic legends is most likely linked to those jinn who fly through the air.

Jinn possession

"For each one are successive angels before and behind him who protect him by the decree of Allah." - Quran 13 : 11

"Behold, two guardian angels appointed to learn a man's doings learn and note them, one sitting on the right and one on the left. Not a word does he utter but there is a sentinel by him, ready to note it." - Quran 50:17-18

"Angels take turns around you, some at night and some by day, and all of them assemble together at the time of the Fajr and 'Asr prayers. Then those who have stayed with you throughout the night, ascend to Allah, who asks them, though he knows the answer better than they about you, 'How have you left my servants?' They reply, 'As we have found them praying, we have left them praying.'" - Bukhari Hadith 10:530, narrated by Abu Huraira

Jinn possession is regarded as a rare occurrence in modern Islam. However, it is still something which can happen and is mentioned in the Quran, with the story of a boy who becomes possessed causing him to convulse in fits of madness. When his mother asks for assistance the jinn is exorcised out from the boy manifesting in the form of a small black cub which runs off leaving the boy cured.

"Of special interest is the version of Ibn 'Abbas in which the Prophet's victory is visible. As soon as he strokes the child's chest (who suffers here from juniin or lamam) with his hand and prays for him, a black cub pops out of the child's mouth and runs away. This reflects the

well-known notion that devils or demons may appear to humans in the form of various animals, such as black dogs, but mainly as serpents and scorpions." - U Rubin Muhammad, Acts of Exorcism.[3]

The alcoholic beverage knows as 'gin' is said to have originated from the word 'genever', a juniper flavoured traditional liquor, made from juniper berries. It was initially made as a medical drink which eventually found its way into the alcohol and spirits industry. However, one can't help but notice the link between the alcoholic spirit called 'gin' and the spirits known as 'jinn'.

The word 'alcohol' is thought to have its origins in the Arabic word 'Al-Khul' or 'Al-Kohl'. Kohl was used in ancient Egypt as an antiseptic, cosmetic and eye-liner. However, it is also thought that 'Al-khul' is the origin for our word 'ghoul', a reference to a body eating spirit. A ghoul is another type of Jinn which is said to hang around graveyards devouring the flesh of humans, whether dead or alive.

"By consuming alcohol into the body, it in effect extracts the very essence of the soul, allowing the body to be more susceptible to neighbouring entities most of which are of low frequencies." - Jason Christoff[4]

Various types of Jinn found in Islam :[5]

- **Jann** : A type of jinn.

- **Marid** : A powerful rebellious demon.

- **Ifrit** : A powerful type of demon associated with the underworld.

- **Ghoul** : Associated with graveyards and consuming human flesh.

- **Si'lat** : Talented shape-shifters often appearing in human form and female.

- **Nasnas** : A creature mentioned as Shaqq in One Thousand and One Nights.

- **Hatif** : A voice that can be heard without discovering the body that made it.

- **Qareen** : A spiritual double of human with a ghostly nature.

- **Hinn** : Supernatural creatures, besides jinn and demons.

- **Shaitan** : Also known as demons who make humans and other jinns sin.

- **Malak** : A jinn who is purely at the service of God/an angel.

Spirit possession within Catholicism

"The great mistake of many people … is to imagine that those whom death has taken, leave us. They do not leave us. They remain! Where are they? In the darkness? Oh, no. It is we who are in darkness. We do not see them, but they see us. Their eyes radiant with glory, are fixed upon our eyes … Though invisible to us, our dead are not absent … They are living near us transfigured into light and power and love." - Karl Rahner, S.J(Society of Jesus).

The word 'spirit' comes from the Latin 'spiritus' which means 'breath' or breathing. The soul is the animated principle energised by the spirit. Only when God breaths his spirit into Adam does he become a living being.

"It is the Spirit who gives life; the flesh is no help at all. The words that I have spoken to you are spirit and life." - John 6 : 63(ESV)

Although the Catholic Church has no definitive position regarding the existence of ghosts, they do believe in spirits and a spirit realm. The word 'ghost' comes from the German word for spirit 'geist', therefore a belief in spirits is essentially a belief in ghosts. The holy trinity is based around a spiritual realm. God the Father is purely a spiritual being with Jesus as God's son, resurrected in union with his divine spirit after his crucifixion. The Holy Ghost or Holy Spirit is the final aspect of their trinity and the feminine part of this triad, ultimately resembling the three aspects of human conciousness.

"God, the blessed and only Ruler, the King of kings and Lord of lords, who alone is immortal and who lives in unapproachable light, whom no one has seen or can see. To him be honour and might forever. Amen." - 1 Timothy 6 : 15-16 (NIV)

"Now the Lord is the Spirit, and where the Spirit of the Lord is, there is freedom." - 2 Corinthians 3 : 17(NIV)

God the Son, in the form of Jesus Christ, became living flesh and his divine spirit united externally to that human body after the resurrection. Now in spirit form, his kingdom is not of this realm.

Jesus said, "My kingdom is not of this world. If it were, my servants would fight to prevent my arrest by the Jewish leaders. But now my kingdom is from another place." - John 18 : 36 (NIV)

Jesus was conceived by the Holy Ghost/Spirit and born to the Virgin Mary. The Holy Spirit also descended upon Jesus, like a dove, during his baptism. Furthermore, after the Last Supper Jesus promised to send the Holy Spirit to his disciples following on from his final departure.

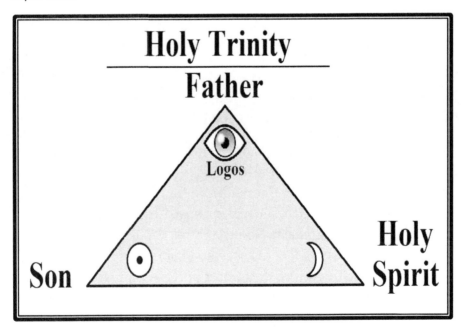

The Christian view of angels and demons, through the Catholic perspective, is relatively simple, as all entities outside our physical reality are classed as spirits. There are good spirits and bad spirits depending upon their relationship to the Creator, and willingness to serve God. All angels are purely spirits, however, they have the ability to manifest themselves into physical form for specific reasons. In the Book of Tobit (part of the Catholic and Orthodox biblical cannon) Archangel Raphael appears disguised as a human travelling companion to Tobit's son Tobiah. The angel calls himself Azarias. Eventually, after curing Tobit's blindness the angel reveals his true identity.

"And now the Lord hath sent me to heal thee, and to deliver Sara thy son's wife from the devil. For I am the angel Raphael, one of the seven, who stand before the Lord." - Torbit 12 : 15 (GNT)

Spirits who made the choice not to serve God were cast out of heaven, these are known as fallen angels, led by Satan or the Devil.

"And the great dragon was thrown down, that ancient serpent, who is called the devil and Satan, the deceiver of the whole world—he was thrown down to the earth, and his angels were thrown down with him." - Revelation 12 : 9 (ESV)

These Malevolent spirits are thought to be behind most , if not all, of the chaos and misery experienced by humanity throughout history. Satan is said to be the prince of darkness and also Lord over this physical material realm.

"We know that we are children of God, and that the whole world is under the control of the evil one." 1 John 5:19

"Satan, who is the God of this world, has blinded the minds of those who don't believe. They are unable to see the glorious light of the Good News. They don't understand this message about the glory of Christ, who is the exact likeness of God. " - 2 Corinthians 4:4 (NLT)

Each fallen angel has a unique quality of mischief and malevolence, trying to entice humanity away from God's divine plan, towards a selfish existence of materialism, devoid of any spiritual awareness and unity with the Creator. It is believed that these fallen angels also have the ability to take on physical form.

"Do not believe every spirit, but test the spirits to see whether they are from God, for many false prophets have gone out into the world." - 1 John 4 : 1 (NIV)

Just as the pneuma was the main driver or motivating force behind our initial physical animation, future spiritual attachments can contribute to this animation as an additional influence as we grow and develop. It is therefore up to the individual which type of spirit they allow within their own triad of consciousness. It is believed by most Catholics, and Christians of other denominations, that bad spirits or those associated with fallen angels go out of their way to entice and seduce humanity into following their deviant nature, pulling us away from God's protection and grace.

"Finally, be strong in the Lord and in the strength of his might. Put on the whole armour of God, that you may be able to stand against the schemes of the devil. For we do not wrestle against flesh and blood, but against the rulers, against the authorities, against the cosmic powers over this present darkness, against the spiritual forces of evil in the heavenly places." - Ephesians 6:10-12 (ESV)

For most Christians, life becomes a constant struggle to keep themselves and their thoughts free from demonic influence on all levels. This is not an easy task, especially in this modern world of competitive division and materialism. Their traditional ways of opposing the forces of darkness are becoming diluted as humanity progresses further down the road of globalisation towards the new Age of Aquarius. While most Christians try to avoid any discourse or interaction with demonic spirits they welcome good ones especially the Holy Spirit, which many encourage and aspire into receiving. Prayers and services are designed to facilitate interaction with the Holy Spirit, inviting this Holy Ghost into the minds and hearts of those who participate in these ceremonies. In some cases, the filling or interaction with the Holy Spirit can manifest a number of physical expressions and displays of paranormal activity. Some recipients begin to speak unintelligible utterances known as 'speaking in tongues', thought, by some, to be the language of Angels or the language of the Gods.

"When the day of Pentecost came, they were all together in one place. Suddenly a sound like the blowing of a violent wind came from heaven and filled the whole house where they were sitting. They saw what seemed to be tongues of fire that separated and came to rest on each of them. All of them were filled with the Holy Spirit and began to speak in other tongues as the Spirit enabled them." - Acts 2 : 1-4 (NIV)

So Ananias departed and entered the house, and after laying his hands on him said, "Brother Saul, the Lord Jesus, who appeared to you on the road by which you were coming, has sent me so that you may regain your sight and be filled with the Holy Spirit." - Acts 9 : 17 (NIV)

While the Holy Spirit appears to bestow all that we consider to be good and positive upon those who come into contact with it, any interaction with bad or demonic spirits are thought to corrupt a person's soul, bringing nothing but misery, suffering and ultimately death to that individual. As with the Vodouists, some people who consider themselves to be Christian see no problem in associating and conversing with various fringe spirits, which they believe will help and guide them towards personal goals and ultimately a more fulfilled life. It is forbidden in mainstream Christianity to have any form of discourse with spirits other than those allied with God the Creator. Those who attempt to connect with dead or demonic spirits, in any way and for any reason, are committing heresy, a serious charge within the Catholic Church which, at one time, carried the death penalty. One reason why they are so strict on this matter is because the Apostle Luke made it clear that a great divide was created between those in

Heaven and those whom God threw out, a chasm which cannot be crossed. Therefore, any spirit not within the heavenly realms are regarded an antagonistic towards the Creator.

"But Abraham replied, 'Son, remember that in your lifetime you received your good things, while Lazarus received bad things, but now he is comforted here and you are in agony. And besides all this, between us and you a great chasm has been set in place, so that those who want to go from here to you cannot, nor can anyone cross over from there to us." - Luke 16 : 25-26 (NIV)

From this parable the Church Fathers made the assumption that the spirits of the dead, especially those of good standing, could not pass or connect with the world of the living. Therefore, any form of divination which required the assistance of spirits was viewed as demonic.

"All forms of divination are to be rejected: recourse to Satan or demons, conjuring up the dead or other practices falsely supposed to "unveil" the future. Consulting horoscopes, astrology, palm reading, interpretation of omens and lots, the phenomena of clairvoyance, and recourse to mediums all conceal a desire for power over time, history, and, in the last analysis, other human beings, as well as a wish to conciliate hidden powers. They contradict the honour, respect, and loving fear that we owe to God alone." - Catechism of the Catholic Church, second edition, 2116

"Let no one be found among you who sacrifices their son or daughter in the fire, who practices divination or sorcery, interprets omens, engages in witchcraft, or casts spells, or who is a medium or spiritualist or who consults the dead. Anyone who does these things is detestable to the Lord; because of these same detestable practices the Lord your God will drive out those nations before you. You must be blameless before the Lord your God." - Deuteronomy 18:10-15 (NIV)

Consequently, according to the Catholic Church, anyone wishing to converse with a recently deceased loved one, should only do it through prayer offerings, which are ultimately heard by God the Creator. Your prayers are either heard directly by God or picked up by the saints in heaven and relayed back to God as petitions of prayers presented in the form of bowls of incense.

"And when he had taken it, the four living creatures and the twenty-four elders fell down before the Lamb. Each one had a harp and they were holding golden bowls full of incense, which are the prayers of God's people." - Revelation 5 : 8 (NIV)

According to Catholic principles not everyone who dies has reached the required level of purity in relation to their sins, allowing them to enter heaven. Therefore, every year, following on from 'All Saints Day' on the first of November, a service in commemoration of all those souls who have departed this realm with or without the right credentials are prayed for. This is known as 'All Souls Day'. Prayers are offered in an attempt to clear the way for their ascension into heaven.

"Ghosts are reminders that our brothers and sisters are in need of our prayers." - Father Mark Schmitt

"All Souls Day (November 2) is a time when we particularly remember those who have died. The prayers appointed for that day remind us that we are joined with the Communion of Saints, that great group of Christians who have finished their earthly life and with who we share the hope of resurrection from the dead." - Bays & Hancock 2012, p. 128

Exorcism

The dictionary definition of the word 'exorcism' refers to 'the removing of evil spirits from a person or place by the use of prayer.' This makes perfect sense when the word 'ex-orc-ism' is broken down.

- Ex - 'out of'.

- Orc - 'a mythical creature such as a sea monster, a giant or an ogre of horrid form.' Orcus being the God of the underworld.

- Ism - 'an act, practice or process.'

Exorcism is the religious or spiritual practice of casting out unwanted spirits which have attached themselves to a person, in the form of spiritual possession. This is usually done by either commanding the spirit to leave in the name of a higher power or by persuading it to depart through some form of ceremony or ritual. A formal exorcism within the Catholic tradition is usually carried out by an ordained priest, during which, he will invoke the highest righteous spiritual powers to intervene on his behalf. These include Angels, Archangels, the Saints, the Holy Spirit, Jesus and even God himself, all subjecting bad and demonic spirits to an onslaught of righteous light and godliness which acts as a suffocating repellent prompting the evil entity into upping sticks and leaving. Although most victims of possession are viewed as unwilling participants who have been manipulated by demonic spirits and are therefore not entirely responsible for their actions, there are some instances where the individual has wilfully submitted to the forces of evil. In such rare cases these possessed victims are not always treated with the same level of compassion as those who are considered innocent of all blame. A Catholic exorcism is a serious undertaking, one which can take weeks, months and even years of persistent exorcisms in order to expel a deeply embedded demonic spirit. One prayer often used as a powerful antidote to diabolic possession calls upon the powers of Archangel Michael to drive out any demonic entity, which also protects an individual from bad spirits in general.

"St. Michael the Archangel, defend us in battle. Be our protection against the wickedness and snares of the devil. May God rebuke him, we humbly pray. And do you, O Prince of the heavenly host, by the divine power, thrust into hell Satan and all evil spirits who prowl about the world, seeking the ruin of souls." - Prayer to St. Michael Archangel, attributed to Pope Leo X.

Before a case of exorcism is granted by a local Bishop certain criteria must be met in order to satisfy those members of the Church involved of its authenticity. This includes a careful medical examination to exclude the possibility of mental illness as a root cause. Other indications are taken into account such as speaking in a foreign or ancient language, one which the victim had no prior knowledge of. Supernatural abilities or extraordinary strength, suggesting the victim is under some other external influence. Knowledge of concealed or remote things which the possessed person was not aware of before. Also an aversion to anything considered holy, together with acts of sacrilege and blasphemy. Other signs of demonic invasion can vary depending upon the spirit involved[6] :

- Loss or lack of appetite.
- Cutting, scratching, and biting of skin.
- A cold feeling in the room.
- Unnatural bodily postures and change in the person's face and body.
- The possessed losing control of their normal personality and entering into a frenzy or rage, and / or attacking others.
- Change in the person's voice.
- Supernatural physical strength not consistent with the person's build or age.
- Speaking in tongues the person cannot have learned before.
- Knowledge of past events which the person could not have known about, knowledge of present events which the person has not witnessed or have knowledge about and predictions of future events that become accurate (sometimes through dreams).
- Levitation and moving of objects / things.
- Expelling of objects / things / certain animals.

- Intense hatred / aversion and violent reaction toward religious objects or items.

- Antipathy towards entering a church, speaking Jesus' name, or hearing scripture.

The case of Emma Schmidt (pseudonym (Anna Ecklund)) 1928

This is one of the best documented cases ever to have taken place within the United Stated and probably the Catholic Church as a whole. Within the Catholic Church there is what is known as the 'Order of Exorcism', and when a Bishop confers this order he pronounces the following words :

"You receive the power to place your hand upon those possessed and through the imposition of your hands, the grace of the Holy Ghost and the words of exorcism you shall drive evil spirits out of the bodies of those so possessed." - Begone Satan[7]

Anna Ecklund began life like most other Catholic girls born at the end of the 19th century. Although born in Switzerland, her German parents moved to Marathon, Wisconsin when she was still very young. Records suggest she was an enthusiastic girl, eager and happy to attend church services and participate in events. However, as she began to mature, growing towards adolescence, her father Jakob began to impose his will upon her. He was an abusive drunk who tried to seduce her into having sex with him. Anna's mother had left the family home while she was still very young leaving no record as to who she was or where she went. Consequently, Anna's relationship with her father began to deteriorate. Furthermore, Jakob frequently mocked the Church along with its members and ministers. As Jakob was unable to have his way with his daughter he would instead spend time with his mistress Mina, Anna's aunt, who many believed to be either Jakob's sister or half sister. Mina had a reputation within the town for being an active participant in witchcraft and black magic. Both of them would grow to despise Anna, conspiring together to bring supernatural misfortune upon her. This was when things began to go wrong for Anna.

Previously an active member of the Church, she began to show signs of aversion towards the church and religious objects. At only 14 years old, not only did she show outward revulsion towards the church, which she was now physically unable to enter, she began to take part in bizarre and unspeakable sexual acts. Over the next ten years her behaviour steadily deteriorated which came to the attention of Father Theophilus Riesinger, a Bavarian born Catholic priest, now living in the United States, who specialised in spiritual possession and exorcism. After various meetings and consultations Riesinger deemed her behaviour to be a form of possession and recommended an exorcism to be performed. On June 8th 1908 Anna's first exorcism took place, which for all intents and purposes appeared successful. Few records of Anna's case were made during these early interactions. It is therefore believed that she continued a relatively normal life until her father died, years later, which appeared to trigger an escalation in her unusual adverse behaviour towards the church. This resulted in violent episodes against her spiritual councillor and other members of the church. At this point she began to hear voices in her head which were driving her into fits of despair. After being diagnosed as physically fit by multiple doctors she finally turned once more to the church for help. Over the next few years Anna's church councillors attempted to diagnose her, finding some oddities which they couldn't explain. One of these anomalies was her ability to understand languages which she had not previously known or studied. It was noted that when priests spoke to her in Latin she would foam at the mouth and become enraged. She was also able to identify items which had been blessed, demanding that they be removed from her presence. Finally, in 1928, after many years of assessment, now at the age of 46, Anna was officially deemed to be possessed by her church councillors who once more turned to Father Theophilus Riesinger for help. Once Riesinger appeared on the scene detailed records of Anna's case were made culminating in an internal Catholic Church pamphlet on exorcism entitled 'Begone Satan'.[7]

Father Theophilus Riesinger, the Catholic Church's most experienced exorcist, within the United States, suggested that the exorcism be carried out at a Convent in order to keep the whole episode secret and confidential. The Convent chosen was in Earling, Iowa, as the Pastor, Father Steiger was a life long friend of Riesinger, and would be able to assist him throughout the exorcism procedure while making detailed notes regarding the matter.

On arrival at Earling station, accompanied by a number of priests, although appearing to be her usual self, Anna unexpectedly attacked the priest who had come to meet her. Furthermore, Riesinger, who arrived on a later train, was left waiting at the station for two hours because Father Steiger's new car would not start, and with no obvious signs of mechanical failure, Riesinger put it down to Satan playing games, he later said :

"The Devil will try his utmost to foil our plans". Father Theophilus Riesinger

That night, with all participants present at the convent, one of the nuns, who had prepared some food for Anna, decided to sprinkle holy water over the dish, giving it a blessing. However, when the food was presented to Anna, she began to purr like a cat, refusing to eat any food which had been blessed. This became a common theme throughout her stay, instinctively knowing when her food had been blessed or not.

First exorcism session 18th - 26th August, 1928

The exorcism began on the morning of 18th August, 1928. Both Riesinger and Steiger had attended morning mass before arming themselves with a variety of holy symbols, holy water and scripture. As soon as they entered the room where Anna was staying they began to recite the names of the Holy Trinity. At this point Anna leaped from the bed, slipping through the hands of the nuns holding her down and landed on top of the door. She then flung herself at the wall where she clung on sideways growling like a demented animal throughout the

141

whole ordeal. Startled at first by this, the group, consisting of three priests and several nuns, composed themselves and continued to pray over her, eventually bringing her back down onto the bed. Although Anna had not eaten much prior to her arrival at the Convent and little while she was there, she began to vomit vast quantities of a vile smelling substance. One witness stated after seeing Anna vomit over 20 times in one day said :

"Quantities that were, humanly speaking, impossible to fit inside a normal being."[7]

Throughout most of the first session Anna remained in a semi comatose state while the room filled with a fowl putrid stench of filth. Although unaware of what was unfolding around her, Anna would mutter and speak in various languages predominantly Latin, German or English, other times she would just growl demonic murmurings and animal like noises.

"The evil spirits simply spoke in an audible manner from somewhere within her."[7]

From the outbursts and mutterings Riesinger concluded that Anna was possessed by at least five different demonic spirits.

1. Her Father Jakob

2. Her Aunt Mina

3. Beelzebub

4. Judas Iscariot

5. Lucifer

Along with these five main demonic spirits other lesser evil demons would appear in packs, like wild animals. This process of praying and laying on hands went on for eight days until the group, fearing for Anna's life, suspended the proceedings in order to refresh themselves and to give Anna a rest. At this point Anna was frail, emaciated and pale and the team thought there was a possibility that she may not recover.

Second exorcism session 13th - 20th September, 1928

Second exorcism session 13th - 20th September, 1928

After a few weeks rest Anna's strength had returned to a point at which proceedings could continue. The second session of exorcism began on the 13th September, and as before went on for a whole week. During this session the team were able to gather more information about particular demons possessing her. Riesinger was able to communicate with the spirits using a variety of different languages, each time the demon would answer in the same corresponding language. Beelzebub told Riesinger that Satan had commanded him to possess Anna from the age of 14 and that Jakob, Anna's father had cursed her for not having sex with him, commanding Satan to possess her. Judas Iscariot also came forward and said that he had been instructed to torture Anna and drive her to suicide.

"To Bring her to despair, so that she will commit suicide and hang herself! She must get the rope, she must go to hell!" - Judas Iscariot

Jakob, Anna's father came forth telling of how he spent his life ridiculing the church and throwing off any semblance of faith. However, this on its own was not enough to cast him into damnation. It was his insistence in cursing his daughter that sealed his fate. Now in hell, he continued to scheme against his daughter for shunning his sexual advances. Riesinger concluded that her father was a bitter and twisted spirit possessing his daughter in order to cause as much suffering on her as he could.

Mina, Anna's aunt, told how she was damned, not only for her affair with Jakob, but for the killing of four of her own children, which she undertook with little or no remorse. Mina's disjointed utterances were documented by Riesinger :

"Filled with such bitter hatred and spite that they far surpassed all that had happened so far. Her demeanour towards the Blessed

Sacrament is beyond description. She would spit and vomit in a hideous manner so that both Father Theophilus and the pastor had to use handkerchiefs constantly to wipe off the spittle from habit and cassock. Because of her unworthy communions, it was clear that the Blessed Sacrament, the Bread of Eternal Life, which should have been the source of her eternal salvation, turned out to be unto her eternal damnation. For she tried to get at the Blessed Sacrament with a burning vengeance and hatred." - Father Theophilus Riesinger

As the week progressed Anna's body went from being as light as a feather, almost to the point of levitation, to being so heavy that it sank into the bed sheets bending the metal bed frame. At one point Anna became red and swollen to the point where she was almost unrecognisable, then she would revert back to being emaciated and pale. Once again the group suspended proceedings fearing for Anna's safety. By now the room had become a pit of despair, with a vile, pungent smell of demonic vomit and filth to which no one could remain close to for any period of time.

Throughout the first two sessions the demonic spirits had been taunting various members of the team by disclosing personal secrets in an attempt to undermine their confidence. These taunts began to weaken Paster Steiger's resolve, to a point where he began to doubt and question his old friend Father Theophilus Riesinger. The Devil had told Steiger that he would regret his involvement in this affair and the parish would ultimately turn against him.

"I'll incite the whole Parish against you, " The devil said "I will calumniate you in such a way that you will no longer be able to defend yourself. Then you will have to pack up and leave in shame and regret." - "I cannot harm God directly, but I can touch you and his church. Just wait until the end of the week! When Friday comes then..."[7]

The devil abruptly ended his sentence ominously, leaving a bad omen hanging in the air.

The following Friday Paster Steiger was called to a home visit to read the last rights to a dying woman. Although it was a journey he had undertaken many times, knowing the road well, he still took extra care in view of what the demons had told him. On his return a black cloud appeared to descend over the road at a notoriously difficult spot, where a bridge crossed over a ravine. Consequently, the car smashed into the barrier on the side of the bridge and overturned, leaving the car hanging precariously over the edge. Fortunately Steiger was able to crawl out from beneath the wreck helped by a farmer who had heard the crash from a nearby field. The Farmer first took the Paster to see a doctor who gave him the all clear before heading back to the Convent. When Steiger entered the room in which Anna was staying laughter erupted out of nowhere.

"I certainly showed him up today. What about your new auto, that dandy car which was smashed to smithereens? It serves you right!" - Demon[7]

Following this incident Paster Steiger seemed to lose his nerve and deemed himself unfit for most of the final session. While he found other work to do around the parish, he continued to support and assist Riesinger whenever he could.

Final exorcism session 15th - 22nd December, 1928

All the lesser demons had been chased out during the two previous sessions, Riesinger's final battle was with the four main perpetrators of Anna's possession. He was determined to complete the process which he had begun four months prior. Not only was it a battle to literally save Anna's life, it had become a personal battle between himself and all those demonic entities which infested the dark caverns of the underworld. He threw himself whole heartedly into the prayers, leaving no free time for the demons to regroup, unleashing an onslaught of Divine energy blasting bolts of righteous light into the very heart of Satan's lair. A breaking point came when Anna appeared to almost levitate off the bed, with only her heels touching the sheets. At this point Riesinger summoned all the power and strength he could from within himself, commanding the demons to leave at once in the name of Jesus Christ and the power of God's heavenly kingdom. "Be gone Satan and take all your demons with you."At this point Riesinger saw a vision of Lucifer and Beelezebub standing in the corner of the room seething with rage and unable to harm the priest. He described Lucifer as tall with matted black fur on his lower hoofed body. At the end of this vision the room rumbled and shook with a crashing of energy before falling silent. Anna collapsed back onto the bed eventually opening her eyes with a brief smile saying. "My Jesus, mercy praise be Jesus Christ."

Over the following months and years Anna's life returned to relative normality, with only minor bouts of demonic intrusion which she was able to deal with herself. She visited the Convent four months after the exorcism, only to find that most of the staff who took part in the ordeal had applied for transfers, feeling that they were unable to stay in the convent with such disturbing memories. Theresa Wegerer, housekeeper to Father Steiger gave the following testimony :

"I was a witness to almost the whole period of the exorcism of the Earling possession case and I can truthfully say, that the facts mentioned in *Begone Satan* are correct. Some of the scenes were even more frightful than described in the booklet. There is not the slightest doubt in my mind, that the devils were present and I will never forget the horrible scenes, vile, filthy, and dirty, as long as I live." - Theresa Wegerer

Be Gone Satan

Spirit Possession in Buddhism

Buddhists are very much in tune with the concept of reincarnation, they hold the view that consciousness moves through cycles of evolving and devolving expressions, experiencing various realms depending upon their Karmic disposition and actions during previous incarnations. The consciousness never dies, it continues in one form or another, with the aim of reaching higher levels of awareness towards enlightenment. Through the teachings of the Buddha (dharma), a person has the potential to move higher up the spiritual ladder in their next rebirth. The Buddha's teachings are considered so profoundly wise that they not only resonate and apply within this physical earthly realm, but also have an impact throughout other realms, both higher and lower; enabling the spirits and entities who inhabit these other realms to improve their own karmic potential, thereby allowing them to also progress even higher in their next rebirth. Similar to the Muslims, spirits within other realms who appreciate the Buddha's teachings can be persuaded into promoting and supporting them. Throughout his life, the Buddha had many encounters with spirits, most of whom could see the great wisdom and benefits of his teachings. As a result many spirits would support the Buddha is all his endeavours.

Six Realms of Incarnation

Heaven & Devas

Demigods Spirits

Human

Animals

Hungry Ghosts

Hells

In Buddhism, Hinduism and Jainism the 'Naga' or 'Nagi' are serpentine demigods who can take on a variety of forms, sometimes as human and sometimes as multi-headed cobra. They are thought to frequent watery places, such as rivers, lakes and marshes and the more hoods they display the more powerful they are said to be. Once Buddha reached enlightenment he sat under a bodhi tree to meditate for several weeks. During the fourth week a tremendous downpour occurred, the heavens darkened and the rivers began to overflow.

However, seeing the possibility of danger to the Buddha, Mucalinda, king of the Naga serpents appeared and began to lift Buddha up upon his great serpentine body, coiling underneath Buddha while protecting him from the rain with a canopy of cobra heads. This famous story of spiritual protection by the Naga elevated the Buddha to even greater heights of credibility and prestige. Furthermore, with the spirits holding the Buddha is such high regard it was easy for the people to follow suit.

Mucalinda, King of the Naga Serpents

With so many different spirits and demigods respecting and protecting the Buddha, it became a common practice for followers of Buddhism to bring figures, images and statues of these various spirits into the temple grounds as a mark of respect to them, believing that their presence would protect the area from unwanted malevolent spirits. The central focus is always that of the Buddha with the good spirits placed around the perimeter of the temple complex, where visitors can present offerings and prayers as they make their way towards the Buddha at the centre. In Thailand it is also common to see spirit houses outside homes, hotels, offices and many other buildings throughout the country. These are ornate miniature houses set on pedestals, designed as a focal point for prayers and offerings to good spirits in the vicinity. With the protection of good spirits, it is thought bad ones will leave the people alone.

Spirit Houses, Thailand

As Buddhists believe in rebirth within one of many realms, it is possible that we may return as an animal, a hungry ghost or even as one of many people sent to hell for a period of torment. Buddhists do not regard any incarnation or experience as permanent, instead they view all these realms as interconnected, perpetually evolving and revolving. A person may die and be reborn into the realm of the demigods or even as a hungry ghost, unable to satisfy their basic needs. Even the Gods in heaven are deemed to hold temporary positions from which they could devolve back into human form in order to fulfil some purpose or resolve some karmic discrepancy.

Hungry Ghosts are beings driven by intense emotional needs in a base animalistic fashion. Also known as 'Preta', these hungry ghosts experience suffering on a level far greater than that of humans, particularly in relation to extreme levels of hunger and thirst. The concept of the preta originated in India and was adopted by many East Asian religions through the spread of Buddhism. The suffering ghost is thought to be in a transient state between death and their next karmic reincarnation. A state which can be helped by prayers and offerings from the land of the living. To become a preta a person must have done some bad things during a previous life to accumulate such bad karma. Corrupt, deceitful, jealous and greedy behaviour all have the potential to lead a soul towards preta, together with killing, stealing and sexual misconduct. An ancient story tells of a rich man who made his wealth from travelling about selling sugar cane juice. One day a monk appeared at his house in search of juice to help alleviate an illness. The rich man, who was on his way out at the time, instructed his wife to give the monk what he needed in his absence. Instead of doing what was asked of her, the wife secretly urinated in the monk's bowl, added sugar cane juice and gave it to the monk. The monk, suspecting foul play poured out the contents onto the floor and left. Consequently, when the wife died she became a hungry ghost. Many legends relate to greedy women who refused to give away even small amounts of food, all of which became preta. The world of the preta is different to ours, in the sense that it is full of the most filthy and vile substances known to man. It is said that they occupy the same space as us humans but we cannot see them. While we look into a river and see our reflection, the hungry ghost sees a stream of puss, vomit and excrement. Their necks are pencil thin and their bellies are big and round, expressing their craving for sustenance while still being unable to satisfy these desires. It is said they will go to desperate lengths to satisfy their hunger by congregating around public toilets to feed off human waste. It is therefore necessary for us humans to make prayer offerings and gift sacrifices in an attempt to alleviate the pretas suffering which can also help them towards a new rebirth. Chinese and

Vietnamese Buddhists believe that the ghosts of their ancestors are given permission to visit the world of the living at certain times of the year, a time when the gates of the lower worlds are opened for hungry ghosts to roam the earth seeking food and entertainment. In these countries ghost month is celebrated on the 15th night of the 7th month. This falls on a full moon at the start of harvest season, a time when the first portions of the harvest are offered to dead ancestors and ghosts. Although many of these souls have been sent into a period of suffering, the Buddhists do not judge them, instead they offer food and gifts in an attempt to better their chances of a new rebirth. Together with food, paper gifts are burnt as offerings to make their lives more comfortable. Paper houses are burnt, along with paper cars, televisions and paper money known as 'hell money'. This hell money is considered as valid currency throughout the underworld, helping the ghosts to buy things they need. Tables are set during ghost month with food and gifts. Seats are left empty for the ghosts to sit in and entertainment is provided with night shows at high volume, believing all this will attract their attention. Furthermore, all the seats in the front row are left empty for the ghosts to congregate and have the best view.

Hungry Ghost & Monk

Hungry Ghosts in Public Toilets

According to Dr Yeshi Dhonden, a Tibetan traditional medicine doctor, who served the 14th Dalai Lama from 1961 to 1980, he suggests that spirits have the ability to make a person sick. Saying that spirits such as the naga can harm you through the mind, by directing malevolent thoughts which have the potential to create illness. As some nagas dwell in places like springs, groves and forest areas, if someone comes along and pollutes the spring or chops down trees, which could be home to the naga, they may harm you in retaliation. Once a person falls sick, due to spirit influence, a Lama is required to determine, using divination, what type of spirit is causing the problem, after which various ritual practices and counter measures can be administered. Sometimes the Lama will analyse a person's urine to determine the type of spirit involved and the course of action to be taken. Dr Dhonden points out that there are many different types of spirits with the ability to effect people in many ways :

● **Insane maker** : The mind of the entity merges with the mind of a person causing them to act crazy.

- **Forget maker** : The spirit manifests dementia in a person causing them to become unresponsive, showing no interest in the outside world, appearing detached from everything.

- **Mommo** : This type of spirit makes a person happy, often hysterical, laughing for no reason.

- **Roving Spirit** : People possessed by this spirit find they can't sit still, they are always on the move and restless.

Buddhists believe there are three protective deities or bodhisattvas surrounding the Buddha, each one symbolising one of Buddha's many virtues.

Vajrapani	Manjushri	Avalokitesvara
Protects Buddha & Manifests Buddha's Power	Manifests Buddha's wisdom	Manifests Buddha's compassion

During the early development of Buddhism, ancient Buddhist miracle workers such as Padmasambhava, also known as Guru Rimpoche, tamed a number of demons many years ago turning them towards the teachings of the Buddha to become dharma protectors and fierce guardians of Buddhism. True Buddhists do not view malevolent spirits as demons like most western religions they are seen instead as alternative expressions of energy, deities with power to be worked with. There is no notion of absolute evil in Buddhism or most of the other Asian religions. It is entirely up to the skill and compassion of the practitioner who ultimately determines the outcome of each encounter. The Buddha trumped and outsmarted the king of all demons 'Mara', who is essentially the personification of the forces antagonistic to enlightenment. Mara tried to seduce the Buddha with visions of beautiful women, who were said to be his daughters. However, Buddha was able to resist these temptations as he overcame his own inner demons of greed, aversion and ignorance. All classes of beings including those in the lower realms such as demons, ghosts and animals can improve their karmic placement by attaining a higher birth in their next incarnation. As demons are part of nature's oscillating order it is far better to be on good terms with them than to be antagonistic, showing little respect. The Buddhist's moral system has developed from a realisation of truth regarding the interdependence of all beings while promoting virtue and compassion throughout all realms.

Tibetan Oracles

Within Tibetan Buddhism, there is a tradition, where mediums, known as oracles, invite one of many mundane gods, with whom they have established a relationship, to take possession of their bodies. The main purpose behind this interaction is to act as a conduit for healing and council, where the spirit takes over the oracle's senses in order to drive out unwanted spirits from those seeking help and to offer advise on numerous topics. Oracle possession is widespread throughout Tibet, Nepal and the Indian Himalayas. These mundane gods and spirits are known to be volatile characters with supernatural powers beyond those of humans. This is why oracles who develop good relationships with their spirits are able to utilise some of these supernatural abilities when helping people. Mundane gods and spirits are often associated with particular locations, however the spirits worshipped in monasteries and temple grounds are generally considered to be of higher rank than those found out in the wild. The ones of very low rank are thought to be malicious spirits or even demons, prone to harming humans for lack of food and a place to live. It is believed that if people appease these bad spirits by providing them with offerings they will become protective spirits as long as the offerings are forthcoming. Spirits who have achieved enlightenment are referred to as 'supramundane', many of which protect the Buddha. Oracles within monasteries are considered superior to those out in the provinces and villages, because the calibre of the spirits they interact with are much higher ranking. As is the case throughout nature, there is always someone greater or lesser than oneself no matter which realm they find themselves in. Therefore, there will always be a wide variety of spirits both benevolent and malevolent with supernatural potential. When possession takes place the oracles go into a trance like state where they shake, sway and speak in different voices. Most oracles have no recollection of the possession once the spirit enters their body and takes over their senses. It is believed that oracles are chosen by the gods who initiate the relationship with a phenomena known as 'god sickness'. Once this occurs, the novice oracle is taken to one side by senior oracles or lamas who will guide and train the new recruit. The initiate has to be prepared through a purification process in order to successfully act as a channel for the gods and spirits to communicate through. Once the oracle has perfected their craft, developing deep trusting relationships with a variety of spirits they set about offering their services to the community. Many oracles will dress for the possessions while standing by an alter containing offerings to the gods, Buddha and various deities. Incense is usually burnt surrounded by a variety of oracular paraphernalia including the oracles scrying mirror, a mirror used for divination allowing the oracle to see hidden aspects of other dimensions both past, present and future. When a patient comes to the oracle for healing, a common cure is for the oracle to suck disease causing matter from the client's body with a thin metal pipe. The pipe does not pierce the skin, as matter is thought to enter the pipe through the power of the spirits. The oracle also blesses the effected area by blowing or spitting on it, oil too is often used as an ointment. The matter extracted from the client's body usually comes in three forms, a jelly like substance, a stone or a piece of flesh. If a stone appears it will be given back to the patient, if jelly appears the oracle will get the patient to wash the substance from the oracle's hands. However, if flesh appears the oracle will ingest the matter as an offering to a spirit animal who often accompanies the main god or goddess possessing them. The most senior oracle in Tibet is the state oracle, also known as the 'Nechung Oracle'. Prior to the annexation of Tibet by the People's Republic of China, the Nechung Oracle was also the head of the Nechung Monastery in Tibet. He is now in exile in Dharamsala, India, along with the 14th Dalai Lama.

Tibetan State Oracle in a Trance

While malicious spirit entities appear to be a common cause for many ailments, karma is also regarded as a cause of disease. In such cases Buddhist rituals and recitations are used to aid these problems as a way to balance out bad karma, and to clear the air of unwanted guests.

It is worth pointing out that Thai Buddhism is practised by 94% of the 69 million people living in Thailand and is a country which attracts around 40 million tourists each year as a favourite holiday destination due to its unique style and traditions. Known for its great hospitality as the 'land of smiles', it is a country which has kept its independence throughout the colonial conquests and wars over the past few centuries. A country which is still ruled by a Dhammaraja (a king who rules his people in accordance with Dharma and the teachings of the Buddha). One can't help but speculate that maybe the number of temples and spirit houses throughout the land have kept enough good spirits happy and content that they, along with the Buddha, protect the country and the majority of its citizens from harm, preserving their unique traditions and way of life.

Incense

Incense is an aromatic substance which releases fragrant smoke when burnt. The name comes from the Latin word 'incendere' which means to burn. It has been used for thousands of years to deter malevolent spirits and appease the gods with its pleasant smell. Evidence of its use goes all the way back to ancient Egypt, where resin balls have been found in many pre historic Egyptian tombs. Various combinations of herbs and substances are used to generate the required fragrance which will burn steadily with a self sustaining ember. Thought to have originated as an aid in healing ceremonies, not only to ward off unwanted spirits but to rid the air of mosquitoes and other airborne pests together with any foul odours present. Some common materials used to make incense sticks are typically plant based including a variety of resins, barks, seeds, roots, and flowers. These vary according to each region and the type of plants and barks available. A combustible base mixture is added to a fragrant mixture to produce the desired result. Common ingredients used are as follows :

- Cinnamon, Frankincense, Musk, Myrrh, Patchouli, Sandalwood.

Used extensively throughout India during Hindu ceremonies and Buddhist cultures, the pleasant fragrance produced has a practical role in various ceremonies and gatherings. At funerals incense would mask the smell of rotting corpses and also the body odour of those paying their respects. The Chinese began to use incense over 4000 years ago in religious practices as an aid in worship. This reached a peak during the Song dynasty (960 - 1279), with numerous buildings constructed specifically for the burning of incense. This practice also spread to Japan, used extensively throughout the country during the 15th and 16th centuries. When incense sticks are made uniformly they also make good time keeping aids, large ones for long periods. Most of the incense sticks used in China are odourless, as it is the smoke which is important to them for carrying their prayers up into the heavens. The burning of frankincense is an ancient practice thought to have come from the Celts who used it to ward off ghosts and demons and to protect them from illness.

In the Good News Translation of Tobit 6, where Tobias catches a fish, the Archangel Raphael explains how certain parts of a fish can be used to chase away bad spirits when burnt.

So Tobias and the angel started out toward Media, taking Tobias' dog along with them. They walked on until sunset, then camped by the Tigris River. Tobias had gone down to wash his feet in the river, when suddenly a huge fish jumped up out of the water and tried to swallow one of his feet. Tobias let out a yell, and the angel called to him, "Grab that fish! Don't let it get away." Then Tobias grabbed the fish and dragged it up on the bank. "Cut the fish open," the angel instructed, "and take out its gall bladder, heart, and liver. Keep these with you; they can be used for medicine, but throw away the guts." Tobias did as the angel had told him. Then he cooked the fish, ate part of it, and salted the rest to take along with him. The two continued on together until they were near Media. Then Tobias asked, "Azarias, my friend, what diseases can be cured by this gall bladder, heart, and liver?" The angel answered, "The heart and liver can be burned and used to chase away a demon or an evil spirit that is tormenting someone. The attacks will stop immediately, and the person will never be troubled again. You can use the gall bladder to treat someone whose eyes are covered with a white film. Just rub it

on his eyes and blow on the film, and he will be able to see again." - Tobit 6 : 1-8 (GNT)

The ability to interact with entities from various other dimensions appears to be a common theme running through almost all ancient civilisations and religious groups. Is it the case that those who consider themselves as ruling classes try to outdo one another by forming relationships with ever more powerful and dangerous spirit entities in the hope of gaining more power for themselves and through supernatural alliances ultimately dominate and control the world? The danger inherent with this is that these competing factions will not stop until they have brought forth an alliance with the Devil himself, the pinnacle of evil which can only lead in one direction, that of hell on Earth, for the Devil is the ultimate deceiver and those who follow him will reap accordingly. And as various factions within the elite secretly perform their dark perverted rituals we as unwitting citizens, of each nation, will be expected to participate, pulled along and exposed to their sinister objectives and ritual sacrifices as they appease and compete with their chosen demonic forces and dark entities.

Elite & Demonic Rituals

Notes for chapter 5

1) Haitian Vodou, Wikipedia,
https://en.wikipedia.org/wiki/Haitian_Vodou

2) Jinn, Wikipedia,
https://en.wikipedia.org/wiki/Jinn#:~:text=Jinn%20is%20an%20Arabic
%20collective,are%20concealed%20from%20the%20senses%22.

3) U Rubin Muhammad, the exorcist, JERUSALEM STUDIES IN ARABIC
AND ISLAM 30(2005), aspects of Islamic-Jewish polemics. THE HEBREW
UNIVERSITY OF JERUSALEM THE FACULTY OF HUMANITIES. Page 100.
http://www.urirubin.com/yahoo_site_admin/assets/docs/Exorcistredu
ced.86222830.pdf

4) Jason Christoff, Alcohol and spiritual possession, Christoff Health,
2017. https://www.jchristoff.com/alcohol-and-spiritual-possession/

5) Types of Jinn in Islam, Wikipedia,
https://en.wikipedia.org/wiki/Types_of_Jinn_in_Islam

6) Exorcism in the Catholic Church, Wikipedia,
https://en.wikipedia.org/wiki/Exorcism_in_the_Catholic_Church

7) Rev. Celestine Kapsner, O.S.B., Begone Satan, 1935, Edited by Br.
Sean, a choir monk, 2008 from an html file at ewtn.com.
https://archive.org/details/BegoneSatanASensationalExpulsionOfTheD
evilWhichOccurredInIowaIn/BegoneSatanbyKapsnerOSB

Chapter 6. Karma

The philosophical concept of Karma, which is thought to have originated from various schools of Indian religious philosophy, regard it as a spiritual principle of cause and effect. Where both a person's actions and intentions (cause) have an influence on their future (effect). The earliest reference to the concept of karma appears in the *'Rigveda'* (ancient Indian collection of Vedic Sanskrit hymns) 1500BC. This limited example is later expanded upon in the *'Upanishads'* (late Vedic Sanskrit texts). South Asian traditions differ from Abrahamic religions as their laws of karma act outside the judgement of the Divine Creator.

Whether these karmic repercussions take place during a person's immediate life or a future lifetime is all part of nature's way of keeping its energetic equilibrium in balance. The principle of what goes around comes around is tied in with reincarnation, because without alternative dimensions and ways to express this karma, it would have to manifest balance during one lifetime, which, as we all know, does not always happen. Consequently, if a person performs good deeds and intentions during their lifetime, they will essentially gain karmic credits and move upwards in conscious development. However, if their lives were corrupted by bad actions and intentions their credit score would diminish sending them down towards lower forms of conscious awareness like a perpetual game of snakes and ladders. If however, a person accidentally or unwittingly caused harm towards another, overwhelming them with remorse, compassion and regret, their karmic credits should not be effected. But those who's minds are filled with evil intent, who rarely act out their thoughts, are more likely to be karmically effected.

Due to differing opinions concerning the specifics of karma throughout various religions and schools of philosophy a defined concise meaning of the term has not entirely been established, as it has slightly different meanings within various groups. However, the basic principle is the same, being nature's way of balancing good and bad energy throughout the universe working independently of any deity or divine judgement.

With every action, emotion or thought energy is emitted which is either good or bad. These actions or intentions essentially produce seeds which will germinate some time within nature's balancing system. Although actions are important the attitude of the intention makes all the difference. A soldier obeying orders from his superiors, who also, in turn, follow orders in a chain of command, resulting in the mind of the soldier being propagandised into fighting what he considers to be a good war, is likely to have to fight, on the opposing side, a soldier, of a similar age, pitted against him believing he is also defending and upholding his county's sound principles, pressured into killing one another because their superiors tell them to.

The impact on the soldier's karma will greatly depend upon what he is thinking at the moment he fires the shot?

This used to be a problem in early conflicts of the 20th century. However, the modern soldier is trained to be an emotionless killing machine, who does not let thinking get in the way of his task. Their training teaches them to operate on instinct, without having to engage any form of moral cognitive discourse. The corporate world of the modern military industrial complex has compartmentalised each person's role in order to remove moral consequence from the equation, they are all essentially following orders. So how does this effect their karmic standing?

To simplify the concept of karma it can be broken down into four different types :

Sanchita karma : (accumulated karma, (quiver of arrows)). This is the store of accumulated karma from all other previous lives, which become seeds waiting for the appropriate time to germinate. It is thought by many scholars on this subject, that only when this karma is balanced to a point of neutrality that the soul can retire leaving the spirit aspect of consciousness to continue in a state of enlightenment towards nirvana.

Praarabdha karma : (arrow in flight). This is a specific part of a person's karmic debt which is being dealt with during this latest incarnation. When analysing a person's astrological birth chart or performing various forms of divination it is this aspect of karma which can be identified. While the sanchita karma can be compared to a quiver of arrows stored on a person's back the praarabdha karma would be the arrow in flight which has just left the bow.

Kriyamana karma : (instant karma). This is considered to be instant karma generated from this lifetime due to the actions and intentions of our free will. Although some kriyamana karma brings relatively instant karma of either justice or gifts others are stored for future rebirths, therefore kriyamana karma is divided into two types.

1) Arabdha Karma : undertaken

2) Anarabdha karma : Dormant, stored

To understand these two types of kriyamana karma a good example would be a situation where two people commit a robbery, only one of them gets caught and sent to jail (arabdha karma). However, the other robber continues his life where sometime in the future he experiences (anarabdha karma).

Aagami karma : This is considered to be the accumulative karma created during this present life, which if unresolved before we die crosses over into future rebirths.

The concept of the archer to describe the various types of karma is an ancient one which still helps to clarify the different types of karma to this day.

"The Archer has already sent an arrow and it has left his hands. He cannot recall it. He is about to shoot another arrow. The bundle of arrows in the quiver on his back is the Sanchita Karma; the arrow he has shot is Praarabdha Karma; and the arrow which he is about to shoot from his bow is Kriyamana Karma. The result of the arrow that he is about to shoot is the Aagami Karma." - Vadic literature

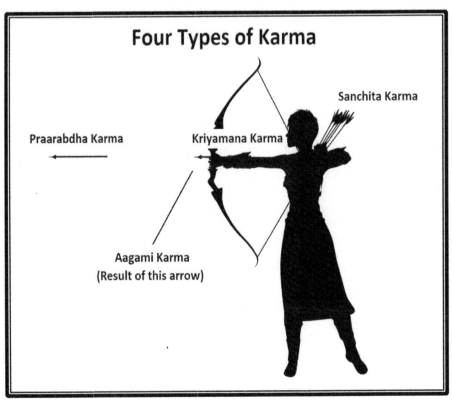

Four Types of Karma

Sanchita Karma

Praarabdha Karma

Kriyamana Karma

Aagami Karma
(Result of this arrow)

"Not even death can wipe out our good deeds." - Buddha

"If you give a good thing to the world, then over time your karma will be good, and you'll receive good."- Russell Simmons

"Men are not punished for their sins, but by them."- Elbert Hubbard

"Karma comes after everyone eventually. You can't get away with screwing people over your whole life, I don't care who you are. What goes around comes around. That's how it works. Sooner or later the universe will serve you the revenge that you deserve."- Jessica Brody

"Realize that everything connects to everything else."- Leonardo Da Vinci

"Don't waste time on revenge. The people who hurt you will eventually face their own karma."- Author Unknown

"No need for revenge. Just sit back and wait. Those who hurt you will eventually screw up themselves and if you're lucky, God will let you watch."- Author Unknown

"One who previously made bad karma, but who reforms and creates good karma, brightens the world like the moon appearing from behind a cloud." - Buddha

Karma can also be divided up into another three basic types :

● Physical : Activities of the body.

● Verbal : Actions of the mouth.

● Mental : Activities of the mind and will.

The law of karma, 'what goes around comes around', is as real as Newton's third law of motion, in which he states 'for every action there is an equal and opposite reaction'. This is all part of nature's balancing act in which we as individuals or as collectives play our parts and influence things.

In Buddhism it is important that thoughts, words and deeds correspond with one another in a constant manner. There is also individual karma and common karma. In the latter all people within a group or nation can share in the causes and effects, good or bad, leading to either social improvements or national disasters. Whoever rules the group or nation has a responsibility to those being governed. According to the Manu Samhita,[1] an ancient legal text and constitution among many Dharmasastras of Hinduism, the king receives 1/6th of the collective karma of those he rules over. It is therefore in the king's interests to treat his subjects well and to benefit from the good karma generated.

"A king who (duly) protects (his subjects) receives from each and all the sixth part of their spiritual merit; if he does not protect them, the sixth part of their demerit also (will fall on him)." - Manu Samhita Chapter 8, no 304

"A king who does not afford protection, (yet) takes his share in kind, his taxes, tolls and duties, daily presents and fines, will (after death) soon sink into hell." - Manu Samhita Chapter 8, no 307

"They declare that a king who affords no protection, (yet) receives the sixth part of the produce, takes upon himself all the foulness of his whole people." - Manu Samhita Chapter 8, no 308

"Know that a king who heeds not the rules (of the law), who is an atheist, and rapacious, who does not protect (his subjects, but) devours them, will sink low (after death)." - Manu Samhita Chapter 8, no 309

Throughout history many civilisations, kingdoms and regimes have met their final doom and collapse at a time when things appeared to be stable and prosperous, yet, nevertheless, theses societies were decadent and deteriorated rapidly and unexpectedly. Although these collapsing societies appeared to happen unexpectedly by many who witnessed them, they were not unexpected by those who understood the universal law of karma.

Certain aspects of a society along with its cultural and moral coordinates have the potential to manifest a significant karmic reaction. The Roman Empire is a good example of a civilisation which collapsed under its own karmic retribution. During its final stages egotism and selfishness plagued its ruling classes, together with a greater discrepancy and inequality between the rich and poor. Many of Rome's citizens became repulsed by the vulgar extravagance displayed by the very wealthy. Furthermore, they had also developed a widespread obsession with all forms of deviant and perverted sex. The city of Pompeii was itself a huge resort for this kind of licentious living and sex, and, as history tells us, the city was buried under tons of volcanic ash from the eruption of Mount Vesuvius in 79AD.

"Pompeii is believed to have had around 25 brothels. [...] Price lists indicate that prostitution services were generally cheaper in Pompeii than other parts of the Roman Empire. On one of the city's central meeting hall walls was the following text: "If you are looking for sweet embraces in this town, you will find that all the girls here are available." Graffiti attests to homosexuality and even to child-rape. [...] The simple evidence shows that in their heyday, Pompeii and Herculaneum were indeed a veritable reincarnation of Sodom and Gomorrah. The evidence further indicates that their destruction represented divine punishment." - Pompeii: Echoes of Sodom and Gomorrah, Watch Jerusalem[2]

When considering the actions and policies of modern nations some appear to have developed sophisticated ways of dispersing karmic retribution as a way of safe guarding their survival. However, although sophisticated tactics are used, I suspect this cannot cover all eventualities and sometime in the future those nations who have imposed their will through force and manipulation, resulting in the deaths and suffering of innocent lives, will eventually receive karmic payback.

Since a person's mindset and intentions play a vital role in their karmic tally when taking any form of action throughout their lives, it is essential for the governing classes to ensure that the mindset of its subjects do not suffer from a conflict of interests towards the country's overall objectives. By compartmentalising almost all aspects of society, modern nations partially protect themselves and their subjects from a karmic backlash, as most people follow orders from their superiors believing them to be honest and sincere, reflecting altruistic aims at the very heart of policy. In this way public servants are able to perform their duty instinctively without questioning their moral stance.

Another mechanism at play is the contract. As almost all organisations and institutions are now run as corporations, the contract is used to relinquish a great deal of karmic backlash by expressing all of its terms and conditions in writing before initiating any venture. Although most individuals do not read government papers regarding future policy or the small print on most contracts, just the action of signing has an impact on the distribution of karma as the government or corporation takes advantage of you. Government structures are designed in such a way as to appear to endorse 'rule by consent' and the sheer act of voting is taken to legitimatise most of their actions. However, governments have a reputation for duplicitous and deceitful behaviour as they look after their own interests at all costs, concealing their true intentions and secret operations from public scrutiny. Any morally dubious action governments undertake, no matter what methods are employed to counteract the karmic backlash, the laws governing the distribution of karma will ultimately find them out and eventually even out the score. The British Empire is a good example of this, as it has a long history of imposing its will upon other people all over the world. While, on one hand, the British Empire attempted to export its version of order, control and prosperity to some of the most remote places on Earth, the vast majority of people who were effected by these impositions did not consent and did not want these new powerful rulers. During Britain's colonial expansion many indigenous cultures suffered cruelty under their new masters. People who, at that time, appeared basic and savage like to the colonialist, but were still part of nature and cousins of the human race. Thousands perished prematurely and therefore have some karmic claim against the British establishment and those who, although following orders, inflicted unnecessary suffering on untold numbers. How this karma will play out upon the British establishment and its people is hard to predict. However, if the nation alters its actions and intentions towards others it may have a chance at internally resolving some of its karmic baggage. Its recent intervention in the Middle East and other aspirations towards globalisation suggest it is still up to its old tricks and may therefore be subjected to nature's wrath.

The British Empire's obsession at promoting the total destruction of Germany during the first half of the 20th century, which ultimately cost the lives of millions, eventually led to the fragmentation and bankruptcy of that empire. A war which many consider to have been unnecessary, especially to the level at which it consumed the whole of Europe and involved almost the entire world. As a result Britain lost many of its colonies to independence, it lost its financial dominance as the world's reserve currency and suffered domestic hardship with food rationing for years afterwards. Although this could be considered as instant karma, the depth of trauma caused to millions of people, on both sides will no doubt have a karmic backlash which will go on for decades and generations.

Thailand, on the other hand, appears to have taken their karmic footprint more seriously than some of those old colonial countries which are now only a shadow of their former selves. The Thai king is listed as the richest monarch on the planet by many publications. It is a country which has kept itself relatively neutral throughout the colonial years of the past two centuries. The majority of Thai people, throughout the country, are very proactive at trying to keep a good karmic balance during their day to day activities, with regular visits to their temples, respect towards spirit houses and adherence to nature's Moon phases and cycles. The overall energy and atmosphere in Thailand appears and feels different to that of the United Kingdom, and as a person who has spent many years in both countries, I suspect, due to its karmic credits, Thailand will inherit a more fruitful, balanced and happier future, than most of those now living in what was once known as Great Britain. Any country which deviates from a sense of moral duty toward one another has the potential to sink further into moral degradation, a situation which could escalate promoting a snowball effect regarding bad karma. It is therefore important to give good moral council and support to each new generation, setting a good standard by example.

Examples of karma

"An experienced trophy hunter died after being crushed to death by an elephant he was tracking down to kill in Zimbabwe. Professional game hunter Ian Gibson was taken down and crushed by a young elephant while he was leading a hunt for them. Reports from the safari indicate Gibson had already killed a mother leopard during the hunt and boasted about his superiority over the animal kingdom." - Bestworthy news[3]

"55-year-old Billy Ray Harris was homeless. He lived on a street corner in Kansas City, holding out a cup and asking passers-by for spare change. But then, one day, his life changed. Sarah Darling passed Harris at his usual spot and dropped some change into his cup. But, unbeknownst to her, she also accidentally dropped in her engagement ring. Though Harris considered selling the ring — he got it appraised for $4,000 — he ultimately couldn't go through with it, and a few days later, he returned the ring to Darling. As a way to say thank you, Darling and her husband Bill Krejci started a fund to raise money for Harris to help him get his life back on track. The fund raised far more than any of them expected — in just three months, people donated more than $190,000." - Today.com[4]

"When Roger Lausier was four years old, he wandered away from his mother during a trip to the beach in 1965. He made his way alone into the water and tried to swim, but an undercurrent pulled him down. He would have died, but a stranger named Alice Blaise dove

into the water and pulled him to shore, where she revived him and saved his life. Nine years later, 13-year-old Roger was out on the same beach when he heard a woman scream, "My husband is drowning!" Roger didn't realize this was a woman he'd met before, but he rushed into action anyway. He jumped onto an inflatable raft, paddled out to the man, and pulled him on, saving his life. Nobody there realized the strange, cosmic coincidence that had just happened until the news reported on it the next day. It wasn't until then that Alice Blaise realized that the young man who had saved her husband's life was the four-year-old boy whose life she'd once saved." - Listverse.com[5]

Ceiling decoration from a Jain Temple in India. The knots represent the interlocking notion of karma.

Importance of forgiveness

The ability to forgive others is all part of the enlightenment process, it is a way to defuse the escalation of destructive energy which has the potential to get out of hand. Forgiving people of their transgressions towards you allows you to keep a calm temperament, protecting a balanced state of mind. And as our thoughts are related to our mind's intentions any negative sentiments towards others has the potential to create bad karma. The need for revenge is a base instinct, an animalistic trait which forms part of a lower entities basic reaction to many situations within the animal realm. As humans we try to rise above these animal instincts in an attempt to elevate our awareness to higher levels of consciousness, and without the ability to forgive, this type of vengeful baggage will only hold an individual back on their path to enlightenment.

"Holding on to anger is like grasping a hot coal with the intent of throwing it at someone else; you are the one who gets burned." - Buddha

"When you hold resentment toward another, you are bound to that person or condition by an emotional link that is stronger than steel. Forgiveness is the only way to dissolve that link and get free." - Catherine Ponder

"Without forgiveness life is governed by an endless cycle of resentment and retaliation." - Roberto Assagioli

"Another method is to consider the fact that the opponent in former rebirths have been a near relation of oneself!" - Buddha

There are basically two aspects to forgiveness, the focal mind's awareness of the situation and the emotional aspect of the transgression. Both need resolving in order for the healing process to start and for forgiveness to unfold. First the conscious mind must make the decision to initiate the forgiveness process which then allows the subconscious emotional part of the mind to heal, which may take some time. As each flashing memory of the indiscretion presents itself, only if that seed is not fed will it perish, and over time the emotional scars created will heal, but he who waters the seeds of bitterness and resentment will never be free from the torment of others. Forgiveness is a process in which the student acts as a fireman dampening any embers left after the initial fire. Only when the mind is free from base instincts can it travel to higher realms.

"But if you do not forgive others their sins, your Father will not forgive your sins." - Matthew 6 : 15 (NIV)

"Love prospers when a fault is forgiven, but dwelling on it separates close friends." - Proverbs 17 : 9 (NIV)

As society operates on a compartmentalised basis, the majority of people going about their business are unaware of the bigger picture or the true intentions of those who lead them. For this reason many who impose the will of the state, on others, are ignorant as to some of its sinister ulterior motives and objectives.

Jesus said, "Father, forgive them, for they do not know what they are doing." - Luke 23 : 34 (NIV)

Notes for chapter 6

1) Manu Samhita, The Laws of Manu, translated by George Bühler in 1886. http://oaks.nvg.org/manu-samhita.html

2) Christopher Eames, Pompeii: Echoes of Sodom and Gomorrah, Watch Jerusalem. 2020. https://watchjerusalem.co.il/856-pompeii-echoes-of-sodom-and-gomo rrah

3) Hunter trampled to death. Bestworthy.com news. https://www.bestworthy.com/professional-hunter-trampled-to-death-by-young-elephant-he-was-looking-to-poach/

4) Lilit Marcus, Man who returned ring no longer homeless. 2013, Today.com news. https://www.today.com/news/man-who-returned-ring-no-longer-hom eless-i-feel-human-8C11044196

5) Mark Oliver, Top 10 unbelievable stories of real life karma. 2017. Listverse. https://listverse.com/2017/06/14/top-10-unbelievable-stories-of-real-l ife-karma/

Chapter 7. Near-death experiences

In 2008 the world's largest near-death experience study was undertaken involving 2060 patients in 15 hospitals throughout the US, UK and Austria. The study set out to examine the range of mental experiences in relation to a person's death. The lead author of the study Dr Sam Parnia, Assistant Professor of Critical Care Medicine and Director of Resuscitation Research at The State University of New York explained :

"Contrary to perception, death is not a specific moment but a potentially reversible process that occurs after any severe illness or accident causes the heart, lungs and brain to cease functioning. If attempts are made to reverse this process, it is referred to as 'cardiac arrest'; however, if these attempts do not succeed it is called 'death'. In this study we wanted to go beyond the emotionally charged yet poorly defined term of NDEs to explore objectively what happens when we die." - Dr Sam Parnia[1]

Among the 2060 patients who took part 46% experienced some form of mental awareness before being brought back into focal consciousness. Some described their experience as fearful even persecutory. Only 9% had a positive experience which was in line with the common perception of a near-death experience. Furthermore, 2% of the group had full recollection of sight and sound more in tune with an out of body experience in which the subjects had full awareness but their point of attention had shifted.

Traditionally, most professionals within the medical profession were led to believe that any form of awareness which takes place after cardiac arrest was due to hallucination or just an illusion. However, during the study one case stood out due to the individual's detailed recollections and visual awareness during the three minutes in which their heart had stopped beating. Usually, once the heart stops the brain will cease to function within 20-30 seconds. Although only a small percentage of those participating in the study showed extraordinary levels of awareness while their hearts had stopped those conducting the study concluded that a great deal more research in this area needed to be done.

"Thus, while it was not possible to absolutely prove the reality or meaning of patients' experiences and claims of awareness, (due to the very low incidence (2 per cent) of explicit recall of visual awareness or so called OBE's), it was impossible to disclaim them either and more work is needed in this area. Clearly, the recalled experience surrounding death now merits further genuine investigation without prejudice." - Dr Sam Parnia

The case of Pam Reynolds

In 1991, at the age of 35, Pam Reynolds, an American singer/song writer began to experience severe head aches, which compelled her to go and see her doctor. After an initial examination the doctor recommended that she go to the hospital for a CAT scan. Once the results had come it was discovered that Reynolds had had an aneurysm (an abnormal bulge or ballooning in the wall of a blood vessel) in her brain, which, if ruptured, would kill her. The hospital recommended an unusually delicate operation in which Reynolds would need the majority of the blood removing from her body in order to render the aneurysm operable. However, before the blood could be removed her body temperature would have to be lowered to below 20 degrees centigrade. Furthermore, her heart was to be stopped and all brain activity flattened while the aneurysm was capped off and isolated. Shutting down the body in this way is akin to being dead as all vital signs of life are suspended, this is referred to in the medical profession as a standstill operation. Due to the delicacy of the procedure, Reynold's body and brain were extensively wired and monitored throughout. This included earphones in both ears emitting audible clicks, many times per second, to check brain function and to obscure any sound coming from elsewhere. Overall Reynolds was in such a deep state of lifelessness that anything which went on around her would not be detected. However, during the operation Pam

Reynolds remembers leaving her body to an elevated point in the room where she could watch and hear everything which went on as she lay there practically dead.[2]

"When I came out of the body there was no pain, no worry, no care. I looked down at my body and knew it was my body. I didn't like looking at the body, that bothered me. But it was a wonderful, wonderful feeling, to be free of it."- Pam Reynolds

Once out of her body Reynolds had a distinct physical sensation which she described as a pulling from just above her belly button. Furthermore, she saw what appeared to be a tiny light in the distance drawing her in. When she was close enough to the light she began to discern her grandmother and uncle, who slowly came towards her.

"I wanted to go into the light, but they wouldn't allow me to do that. There was a time when I realised it was time to return to the body and my uncle took me back through the dark vortex, tunnel looking place, to the body, and I did want to go back, I had my children, I did want to go back." - Pam Reynolds

At this point Pam returns to the operating room, at the same elevated vantage point which she was in before.

"I saw them use a defibrillator on me, I saw the body jump, and when I came into the body my body did this (she jolts back in her seat), and I knew it, I felt it." Pam Reynolds

Fortunately for Reynolds the operation was a great success and she made a full recovery. During the days following the operation she began to recall memories of the event, memories of the delicate procedure to which she was a witness from her new vantage point up near the ceiling. When she relayed this information to the medical staff, they were amazed at how accurate she was, from what they perceived to be a lifeless state with no blood, no heart beats and no brain activity, she described conversations which took place as well as specific tools used during the operation, tools which she would not have seen before. After she had recovered she was asked about her thoughts on dying :

"If death is the worst thing that happens to us, what an incredible thing. If at the end of our lives this is what's going to happen to everyone, I don't see the problem, I really don't get it. I fear pain but I don't fear death." - Pam Reynolds

Near Death Experience

The case of Barbara Bartolome

The near-death experience (NDE) can occur for many reasons, usually through some form of trauma to the body. People involved in accidents or operation complications have found themselves looking at their bodies from an outside perspective, observing events unfold in fine detail. The subject can somehow create an energetic copy of their flesh body, just like in astral projection, where consciousness shifts to a new vantage point. In 1987, Barbara Bartolome a 31-year-old mother of two from Santa Barbara, California was booked to go into hospital for her final discectomy and laminectomy, as part of her back treatment. The day before the operation the doctors wanted to perform a myelogram, a procedure to inject iodine dye into the spine to look for problems on X-Rays. The nurse injected the die into Barbara's neck while she was lying on the X-Ray table. The table was then supposed to lift Barbara steadily upright to allow gravity to aid the die to descend down her spine. This didn't happen. She lay flat and began to hyperventilate; she eventually blacked out and immediately went from her physical body to a place on the ceiling, looking down on herself and the heads of the doctors. From her new vantage point she heard one of the doctors call out "Code Blue". This call is used to indicate a patient requiring resuscitation or otherwise in need of immediate medical attention. From her new position on the ceiling she felt very calm, relaxed and content. Presuming she had died she noticed a presence next to her, a familiarity as though she had always known this presence. While the resuscitation was going on below she began to communicate with this presence, she made it clear she wanted to go back into her body and be with her children again, telling the presence that she had not yet fulfilled her life's purpose and needed to go back. The commotion below intensified, she saw an oxygen mask being placed over her face and a man position a small box on the ledge next to the X-Ray table. She made a comment to the presence about the box, asking what it was. At that moment, she found herself positioned in front of the box looking straight at it. She realized after a while it was a heart monitor. When the box was turned on the line on the screen was flat from left to right, with a continuous beep. Barbara went back to the ceiling to be with the presence. Below her the Neurosurgeon and Orthopaedic surgeon were talking about the delayed arrival of the defibrillator to the X-Ray room. It was taking too long. The Orthopaedic surgeon told everyone to stand clear. He stepped forward towards Barbara's lifeless body and struck her in the chest with the full force of his fists. This procedure is regarded as a last-ditch attempt at shocking the heart into beating again. The second time he struck Barbara's chest, in an instant, she went straight back into her body and opened her eyes. She was so amazed and excited to be back in her body that she was trying to talk under the oxygen mask. The nurse told her to keep quiet because they needed to stabilize her.

After a small bout of silence Barbara started talking again, to the astonishment and disbelief of the doctors and nurses surrounding her, she spoke of being on the ceiling looking at everything unfold below. It was only when she mentioned the conversation between the Neurosurgeon and the Orthopedic surgeon about the defibrillator and how she was struck in the chest twice that the staff stopped what they were doing and stood in amazement at what she was telling them.[3] How could this woman have seen and heard all that was going on around her when her heart had stopped and she was unconscious? Barbara's account of her near-death experience is common amongst NDE's, with thousands of recorded cases all over the world. It appears that while the physical body and 'light' body exist simultaneously our focal consciousness can only occupy one or the other at any given time.

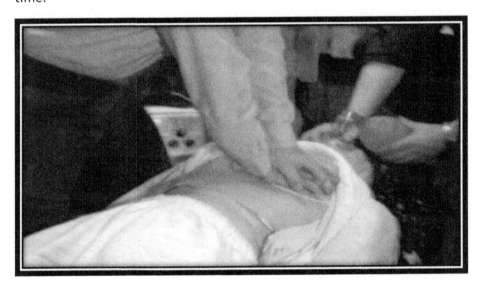

The case of Howard Storm

Howard Storm was born in Newton, Massachusetts in 1946, he graduated from California Berkeley University with a masters degree later to become Professor of Art at the University of North Kentucky, a post which he held for approximately twenty years. In 1985 Storm took a group of students on a field trip to Europe. One afternoon, after returning to his hotel from a morning excursion, he began to suffer from abdominal pains, which progressively got worse and worse. A doctor was summoned and after a basic examination he suspected Storm to have a duodenal perforation, a condition which required urgent surgery, an ambulance was called and Storm was taken to hospital. While in hospital the pain kept intensifying and while the staff searched for a doctor to perform the necessary surgery, Storm had concluded, in his own mind, that he was going to die. He said goodbye to his wife, then passed out and became unconscious. Prior to Storm's near-death experience he described himself as a self centred manipulative individual who was an ardent atheist.

"Realising that I was standing up, that was my first conscious thought, I was standing up and I opened my eyes. I had been right next to the bed that I'd been lying in. The pain wasn't there any more, I was pain free and I was happy. Not only was I pain free, I felt better than I had ever felt my entire life." - Howard Storm

At this point Storm's senses were greatly heightened and his new reality was far more intense than before. He also noticed that his field of vision was almost 360 degrees, as though he could see fully around himself simultaneously.

"It was all very weird, I had awoken to be more alive than I had ever been in my entire life. I saw the bed that I had been laying in and there was a body in it and when I went and looked at the body, in the bed, it looked like me. I refused to believe that it was me, because I was not only alive, but more alive than I'd ever been." - Howard Storm

At this point Storm tried to communicate with his wife, who appeared to be unaware of him standing by the bed. Frustrated by this, he turned to the other patient in the room who also totally ignored him. This made him extremely angry and he shouted "What's going on here, what's happening, what are you doing?" Outside the room was a commotion, some people had gathered in the corridor and they began to call Storm by name, they said "hurry up lets go we've been waiting for you." Storm was in no mood or condition to go with them stressing that he was sick and needed an operation. They said "we know all about you." After a while Storm felt compelled to go into the corridor to see what the commotion was. As he walked into the hallway he felt an eerie feeling and could see that the hallway was completely grey in colour, with a shadowy, creepy overtone. The people there, both male and female adults, kept their distance, they didn't want Storm to see them in the greyness. They beckoned him to go with them and after a while he began to follow them. As they walked down the hallway it became progressively darker and darker, the walls turned into black empty space where only the floor was defined. They walked and walked, time had little relevance in this world and the laws of physics relating to our world didn't apply here. They went far and it seemed as though they had been walking forever. It all became confusing for Storm as he had completely lost his bearings, even if he wanted to turn back he had no idea which way to go. The group he was following grew in size and became increasingly more hostile. "I'm not going with you any further" Storm shouted. They replied "you're almost there." At this point they started to pull and push him in the direction they were all going. Now there was a huge mob of angry grey looking people who were determined to drag and indoctrinate Storm into their dark sinister world.

"It's best defined by what wasn't there which is a world of hopelessness, a world of loneliness but no light. These were people, they weren't demons, they weren't monsters, they were people who had lived in this world, who had lived the same kind of life that I had lived. I hate to admit it but they were my soul mates." - Howard Storm

As his journey into the underworld unfolded Storm realised that all these people had rejected God in a similar way that he had and the further they walked the further away from God they went and all the things God had given them like love, joy, light, and the beauty of creation were absent. This truly was a journey into hell. The atmosphere deteriorated further as the huge mob kicked, punched and abused Storm in a manner worse than any horror or sadomasochist movie, with blood and gore everywhere. He thought he was truly finished and that people who had lived crummy lives on the Earth were sent down the toilet of the universe into a giant cesspool of filth, hatred and godlessness. He also concluded that the whole purpose to these people's existence was to descend as far down into ultimate misery as they could go. After what seemed like an eternity Storm lay on the ground completely deflated in a state of absolute hopelessness, physically and emotionally destroyed. At this point he heard a voice which sounded much like his own, which came from elsewhere, it said "pray to God", to which he thought, I don't pray to God because I don't believe in God. The voice called out again "pray to God". Storm, desperate at this point, searched his memory for some way to communicate with God. Being a life long atheist and antagonist towards religion he was finding it difficult to think of any prayer he could say. As he thought he unintentionally murmured some old recollections of psalms and the Lord's Prayer which he had vague memories of from when he was a child. Upon hearing his utterances the people around him became very angry and began to spit profanities at him, they shouted "There is no God, nobody can hear you and we are going to really hurt you for doing that". Storm found that by mentioning God the crowd around him began to move away and he was now able to repel them. As they moved away, further into the darkness, yelling and screaming at him he began to recollect his childhood memories of Sunday school in which he was told about Jesus, the good man who loves everyone. Storm opened his mouth and yelled "Jesus please save me". At which point a tiny light appeared in the darkness, growing in size, getting closer until it became an intense bright light which consumed him. Hands and arms came out of the light, they reached down and took hold of Storm pulling him up into the light.

"When he touched me, in addition to the physical healing, instead of feeling what I was feeling at that time, I was filled with his love and it

was a much more intense experience of being loved than anything I'd ever known in my entire life and I don't think there are any words in this world to begin to convey how powerful that love is and it's love with an acceptance too." - Howard Storm

With his arms firmly wrapped around Jesus, they both began to move, very rapidly, like a rocket, they left the darkness and headed towards a world of light. Faster and faster they went as this new bright world began to emerge. At this point Storm realised he was heading towards God's house. Feeling unworthy, he thought to himself that he was such a piece of garbage that Jesus was making a serious mistake. Jesus reading Storm's thoughts said "we don't make mistakes, you do belong here", at which point they stopped moving and were now in heaven. Storm was now aware that Jesus was not only able to read his thoughts but was also able to project his voice into Storm's mind, in a form of telepathy. While grappling with this new way of communicating a vision of a beautiful naked woman popped into Storm's mind, which made Jesus laugh. Now Storm was feeling a little uncomfortable knowing that all his thoughts could be seen by others in this place. Storm said to Jesus "this is not good, if you know everything I'm thinking I can't hide anything from you", Jesus replied "well I know it all, I know everything. I have some people I want you to meet." At which point some light beings came over and hung around them in what appeared to be open space. These light beings told Storm that they had recorded his life and wanted to show it to him. To Storm, this sounded like a lot of fun as he began to view his recorded life in chronological order. However, the angels were selective as to what they showed him and what they left out. As his life moved from his childhood into his teenage years problems began to appear which no longer made the viewing fun. He saw his relationship with his father go from bad to worse and he watched as the teenager became more alienated from everybody and everything, withdrawing into his own little bubble, becoming more selfish and manipulative. This part of his life made Jesus and the angels very sad.

185

"There is a common saying in Christianity 'love the sinner but hate the sin', that's exactly, precisely what I was experiencing, that I always felt that they loved me and cared a great deal about me but they didn't like what I was doing with my life because the bottom line was it was harmful to me." - Howard Storm

At his life review, Storm began to realise, although he perceived himself as a victim of the world around him, the reality was that most of his negative behaviour and attitude was of his own doing which had become self destructive. Jesus wanted to show him an alternative, something which he had done which outlined his true potential and real nature. As a teenager, one night, he heard his father enter his sister's room, she was two years his senior. His father began to beat his sister badly, making her cry and scream. Storm wanted to intervene and help his sister but lay on his bed and did nothing. Part of him knew that if he approached his father he would kill him, so he lay there listening to the tormenting sounds of the beating. When the father left, Storm quietly went into his sister's room, where she lay in bed sobbing. He climbed into bed and put his arms around her and held her, she slowly quietened down and began to sleep. The following morning Storm awoke first and with his sister still asleep he scampered out and back into his own room. Jesus turned to Storm and said "now that was beautiful". Throughout the life review they ignored what Storm considered to be his life's achievements instead they focused on his lack of response to other people. All in all he was very disappointed with his life review and at the end Jesus asked Storm if he had any questions, to which he replied "I have a million questions", Jesus said "go ahead".[4]

During his time in heaven Storm asked God "why did you make us?", to which God replied "to love one another." Thinking this would be easy, Storm's whole attitude towards life and his relationships with others changed. After the operation Storm returned back into his body and was now determined to transform his life for the better, taking on a whole new approach, with a more positive attitude. Although Storm was under the impression it would be easy to love others, in practice, he found it to be one of the hardest things he had ever attempted.

The case of Jane Thompson

In 2009 Jane Thompson, a real estate agent, became critically ill due to a kidney stone blockage in her ureter. The result of the blockage prevented the natural release of toxins from her body, instead they poured back into her system infecting her entire blood supply, this resulted in her experiencing septic shock with a loss of consciousness, which propelled her into a beautiful world of love and light.

"I popped out of my body and the next thing I knew I was on the ceiling looking down at myself and everyone around me. I could see that there was no life left in my body. I knew that it was me but I didn't see me there any more. My soul was no longer a part of that shell of a body that I saw on the hospital gurney." - Jane Thompson

From her new vantage point, which she described as very real, clear and focused, she slowly began to drift backwards, floating higher and higher, away from her lifeless body lying in the hospital. Above the hospital she saw little balls of energy buzzing all around her, which she assumed to be souls connected by a thin iridescent line similar to a spider's web as it glistens in the sunlight. This connection of souls represented to her the oneness of consciousness and the way we are all connected. As she progressed upwards and out she entered what seemed like a void or outer space, she did not feel scared as she began to float towards a dark tunnel, she began to move faster and became exhilarated and excited as she travelled through this dark tunnel towards a bright light.

"The tunnel ride was very quick and I popped right out of the tunnel and I was immediately in the white light. The light was so bright and beautiful and powerful that it took me a minute to adjust and understand what was going on there too. As soon as I started to settle into it, I understood that it was heaven." - Jane Thompson

At this point she began to feel an overwhelming sense of unconditional love, a feeling which she had never felt before.

"No matter what I had been through in my life, no matter what I had done. It was just complete love for me. I was bathing in it, it was wrapped all around me and it made me feel valued, appreciated and accepted." - Jane Thompson

Bathing in the light she felt a sense of peace, that everything was OK, that it was all meant to be and was part of a great divine plan. In the light she was getting a healing, all the wounds, scars and holes she had gathered from that life were being filled with love. A great feeling of replenishment making her feel whole again, with a sensation of who she really is and what her soul is all about. She felt in complete union with the white light as though she was the light and the light was her, and any previous feeling of separation from the light was just an illusion.

"I knew that I was dead, I knew that my physical body was no longer working and that I was no longer a part of it and I was fine with it." - Jane Thompson

Now in the light, the life she had just come from seemed like a distant memory, she now felt at home and that there was no other place that could possibly feel as good as this did. She began to contemplate what it would be like to be a mother and have a child, together with an overwhelming sense of everything being OK and all that happens is supposed to happen this way.

"When we are out of our body you have a 360 degree perspective, your not limited to your body, your not limited by your brain, your not limited by your ego because all of that is stripped away and when you do have that broad 360 degree perspective feeling that 'all is well' makes sense. You understand that everything happens for a reason, everything is happening exactly as it should be and there's a lot of peace that goes along with that, and that need to control completely disappears." - Jane Thompson

After some time bathing in the light, soaking up its energy and feeling really good, a crowd began to appear, other souls, making their way towards her. The crowd appeared very friendly and she was not at all scared. Before she got the chance to meet with these other souls a voice come out of nowhere and said "you need to go back". This was not what she wanted to hear, quite the opposite, she did not want to go back, she wanted to stay in this beautiful light. The voice sounded again. It was a loving voice but firm, making it clear that this was not negotiable "you need to go back". Although she persisted with her protests to stay she felt herself being nudged back into the tunnel and very quickly back into her body.

"When I woke up in the pre-op, which was on a weekend and very late at night, I think it was about 9 or 10pm, that part of the hospital was very empty. I knew that I had died, I knew that I had gone into this beautiful white light that loved me, but when I opened my eyes I

was receiving last rights, and I thought, this is odd, it didn't make sense to me." - Jane Thompson

Back in her body, she could observe what was unfolding around her, but was unable to communicate with those giving her the last rights. It was confusing to her and she wanted to tell everyone that she would be OK. If she was going to die she would not have come back and now she is back all is going to be fine. Although her family and surgeon were expecting her to die, the very next day her temperature had dropped from 106 down to 94, the first signs that she was beginning to recover.[5]

Notes for chapter 7

1) Results of world's largest Near-death Experiences study published. University of Southampton, news. 2014. https://www.southampton.ac.uk/news/2014/10/07-worlds-largest-near-death-experiences-study.page

2) Pam Reynolds, Near-death experience. https://en.wikipedia.org/wiki/Pam_Reynolds_case

3) Barbara Bartolome, NDE Radio, Lee Witting, March 26 2014, http://www.youtube.com/watch?v=LVPsqECaUWY

4) Howard Storm interviewed by Matthew Cline, Near-death experience. 2013. https://www.youtube.com/watch?v=VsyWGPoMiMI

5) Jane Thompson, near-death experience interview. 2021. https://www.youtube.com/watch?v=WTESmsletG4

Chapter 8. Psychoactive drugs

Psychoactive or psychotropic drugs are chemical substances which have the ability to alter a person's state of consciousness. By stimulating change within the nervous system our perception of reality, mood, cognitive function and behaviour can all be altered, giving the user a glimpse into other worlds.

"Drugs are able to bring humans into the neighbourhood of divine experience and can thus carry us up from our personal fate and the everyday circumstances of our life into a higher form of reality. It is, however, necessary to understand precisely what is meant by the use of drugs. We do not mean the purely physical craving...That of which we speak is something much higher, namely the knowledge of the possibility of the soul to enter into a lighter being, and to catch a glimpse of deeper insights and more magnificent visions of the beauty, truth, and the divine than we are normally able to spy through the cracks in our prison cell. But there are not many drugs which have the power of stilling such craving. The entire catalogue, at least to the extent that research has thus far written it, may include only opium, hashish, and in rarer cases alcohol, which has enlightening effects only upon very particular characters." - Fitz Hugh Ludlow (1836–1870) in his book *The Hasheesh Eater* (1857)

There is archaeological evidence of the use of psychoactive substances, mostly through plant and plant extracts, going back at least 10,000 years. As cultures evolved, the use of nature's bounty of plants and other naturally occurring substances were used for medical purposes, and because of the interrelationship between traditional spiritual beliefs and spiritual healers these substances were used as part of their religious practices in an attempt to gain subconscious insight as to the underlying cause of many of their illnesses.

The native American Indians used Peyote cacti which contains mescaline, a naturally occurring psychedelic substance which promotes hallucinations similar to LSD. Its use in religious ceremonies dates back almost 6,000 years. Peyote buttons are usually dried and then chewed, they can also be consumed as a drink like tea; other times the buttons are ground into a powder and taken as either a capsule or smoked with tobacco or cannabis. Peyote is considered to be an illegal drug in the United States. However, in 1994 there was an amendment to the American Indian Religious Freedom Act which gave the Native Americans the legal right to use Peyote for religious purposes.[1]

Ayahuasca is another psychoactive substance used throughout South America, described as an entheogenic (Psychoactive) brew. It is a mixture of specific ingredients designed to transcend the conscious mind into alternative states of reality, used primarily in religious and healing ceremonies. The effects of drinking this brew have been compared to that of the near-death experience. The main ingredients used are Banisteriopsis caapi vine and Psychotria viridis shrub or Diplopterys cabrerana as a substitute, together with a variety of other ingredients depending upon the geographical area.

Native American Indian   Peyote   Ayahuasca

Another common and naturally occurring psychoactive drug found throughout the world is cannabis also known and marijuana. This plant has been used for thousands of years as a medicine to relieve a number of unwanted symptoms and also in religious and shamanistic ceremonies. Although cannabis has a long history of use modern governments have proactively tried to restrict its use, suggesting it as a gateway drug into a life of addiction and self abuse. However, many people who use the plant do not agree with their governments stance on its limitations, suggesting alcohol to be far more dangerous to overall health.

Amanita Muscaria also known as fly agaric or fly amanita is a psychoactive mushroom which originated around temperate parts of the northern hemisphere. The Amanita family of mushrooms are some of the deadliest mushrooms in the world, containing chemicals which can kill. Although the Amanita Muscaria is part of this family of mushrooms, its deadly potential is limited. It contains Ibotenic acid and muscimol, both psychoactive compounds. However, it also contains a dangerous chemical called 'muscarine' which is usually present in only relatively small amounts, but because each mushroom contains varying amounts of these chemicals they can still pose a risk when eaten. During the Middle Ages the mushroom was used to kill flies, chopped up and mixed with milk it would attract flies and then poison them. Reindeer have a particular liking for these mushrooms, they will eat them with pleasure, often showing the effects of the mushroom's hallucinogenic properties in their mannerisms. It is said the herdsmen would feed their reindeer with the mushroom then drink the animals urine, which had filtered the dangerous muscarine out via the liver, producing a psychoactive drink. This maybe where the concept of flying reindeer comes from.[2]

Amanita Muscaria and Santa

Accounts of Ayahuasca and hallucinogenic drugs.

A few years ago Brian Rose, an American born former banker and founder of London Real TV took a trip to Costa Rica to participate in an intense experience with Ayahuasca. Although Rose had taken the drug before it didn't have the profound impact that he was looking for and agreed, on this occasion, to try a more concentrated version. Shamans in the old world would consume the ayahuasca brew as part of their traditional ceremonies when trying to gain insight into a person's affairs. Once under the influence the Shaman could see with greater depth and clarity what deep rooted problems could be causing the recipients discomfort. Only relatively recently has the ayahuasca experience been made available to people outside the shamanistic traditions. After taking the brown liquid Brian Rose lay down accompanied by his shaman guide and a couple of friends who had also taken the brew. After some time the drug began to take effect.

"I sat back and had the most profound experience of my entire life. It was slow to set but after it happened I was really in a lot of physical pain and trauma. The medicine was going through my body, I was feeling tormented, I was feeling like I was barely making it." - Brian Rose[3]

At this point Rose connects with an alternative consciousness, as though he had merged with Gaia who was about to reveal to him his full purpose in life and his relationship to all other lifeforms that exist in this reality. He describes it as being totally dissolved with every atom in his body fragmented and spread out into nature. After a few hours in this new state his body began to purge the toxic mixture and made him throw up. When hallucinating under psychotropic drugs time looses its rigidity, it becomes loose and variable, one hour can seem like 10 hours or even 10 days. The thinking processes of the mind race to accommodate thoughts at varying rates, giving the perception of being out of step with time. After the initial purging Rose said his personal version of the 10 commandments were revealed to him, areas in his life which he needed to work on to improve his overall balance with nature and the people in his life which were close to him.

"The first one was just complete dissolution, what it was like to be completely dissolved as a human being. What it was like to be part of nature, what it was like to actually die, the emotions that are involved in that. The whole cycle of life that you see in Gaia whether its animals eating animals or plants decaying into insects and how in fact a human death is not really significant, only in your mind. We are just part of this higher eco system which just keeps going and going."
- Brian Rose

Brian Rose, London Real TV

Each ayahuasca experience is unique to the individual. It is as though they connect to a part of themselves which is timeless, their higher self if you will, and a level of consciousness which sees things holistically.

In a recent interview with Joe Rogan, Graham Hancock, a British writer and journalist discussed his knowledge and experience with Ayahuasca.

"The entities which you encounter, I'm not making any claims about the reality status of these entities, but what I am saying, and it's a fact, that people who work with DMT and ayahuasca do encounter

what they construe to be entities, who communicate with them intelligently." - Graham Hancock[(4)]

Ayahuasca is an example of ancient Amazonian science. From the 150,000 different species of plants and trees living in the Amazon someone in our past discovered that by mixing and boiling Banisteriopsis caapi vine, and the Psychotria viridis shrub together a remarkable drug can be produced which promotes altered states of consciousness. The active ingredient in ayahuasca is DMT which is normally neutralised within the gut by an enzyme called Monoamine oxidase. However, the ayahuasca vine contains a Monoamine oxidase inhibitor which switches off the enzyme in the gut allowing the DMT to penetrate into the blood.

"Ayahuasca means 'the vine of the dead' and what its connected to in South American religious and spiritual thinking is what happens to us when we die." - Graham Hancock

The Tucano people, native to the Amazon have a similar belief in the afterlife as to the indigenous people who lived in the Mississippi valley. Both believed that when ayahuasca is taken the journey embarked upon takes the recipient into the realm of the afterlife. Moreover, on actual death the soul ascends to the constellation of Orion, where it will then transit over to make a journey along the Milky Way which they call the 'path of souls', here challenges and ordeals are encountered in which the soul must account for the life it has just lived. This belief is almost exactly the same as the Egyptian belief concerning the departing soul. Ayahuasca allows us, from the land of the living, to take a glimpse into alternative realms of the afterlife where it is possible to communicate with other entities.

"This is a technology for accessing other levels of reality and it's clear that the native Americans had a number of advanced technologies in this area." - Graham Hancock

Hancock suggests that this Amazonian 'technology', allowing people to transcend this reality, is part of the legacy inherited by various cultures around the world from a remote common ancestor which was more or less destroyed in a global cataclysm thousands of years ago. He also suggests that there could be a connection between the artwork and geoglyphs found in these places and some ancient shamanistic visions.[4]

Ayahuasca Art | Nazca Lines, Peru

Albert Hofmann and LSD

In 1938 Albert Hofmann developed the drug LSD while working on new drugs to stimulate the circulation of blood throughout the body. As a Swiss born chemist, he worked at the prestigious lab of Sandoz, a large pharmaceutical company in Basel, Switzerland. After the creation of LSD-25, the initial studies showed limited promise so the drug was shelved for a number of years. Five years later, in 1943, while synthesising a new test sample Hofmann accidentally absorbed some of the LSD liquid through his skin, making him feel quite strange. He recorded in his notes[5] :

"A remarkable restlessness combined with a slight dizziness." - Albert Hofmann

Concerned with his condition Hofmann went home early to relax and monitor his situation and experience. He wrote :

"Fantastic pictures, extraordinary shapes, with intense kaleidoscopic plays of colour." - Albert Hofmann

The next morning Hofmann felt fine, furthermore, on returning to the lab he decided that he would take a small amount of this new substance, in a loosely controlled experiment. The following Monday, April 19th 1943, Hofmann ingested 0.25mg of LSD-25.

> *LSD EXPERIMENT LOG*
>
> *19/4/1943*
>
> *16:20*
>
> *0.5cc of 1/2 promil aqueous solution of diethylamide tartrate orally = 0.25mg tartrate. Taken diluted with about 10cc water. Tasteless.*

Forty minutes later he began to feel the effects and asked his lab assistant to help him get home. However, due to the restrictions placed on motor transport throughout World War Two, the only transport available was a bicycle. This famous journey, the first cycle trip on acid is now known as 'Bicycle Day' and is now celebrated all around the world on April 19th by fans and followers of Albert Hofmann and LSD.

> *LSD EXPERIMENT LOG*
>
> *19/4/1943*
>
> *17:00*
>
> *Beginning dizziness, feeling of anxiety, visual distortions, symptoms of paralysis, desire to laugh.*

At home, Hofmann was able to totally absorb his experience. His family where away for the week allowing him to fully explore his profound psychotropic experience unmolested. At one point, as he lay on his bed, he describes how his conscious perspective was lifted up and out, towards the ceiling, where he was able to view what he thought was his dead body. Colours became vibrant and vivid forming kaleidoscopic images together with hallucinations of all kinds of magical and wonderful shapes. To his surprise he woke up the next morning feeling remarkably refreshed, like a rebirth, he went outside into his garden to find everything was sparkling with life.

Although the drug did not work as a circulatory stimulant Hofmann and his colleagues at Sandoz came to the conclusion that the drug had great potential as a tool for studying how the mind works.

"Each individual who experiences LSD enters another reality. He enters another world. Seemingly even more real than actual reality. Until that day, I had always thought there was only one reality. Suddenly I was experiencing another." Albert Hofmann

"LSD is just a tool to turn us into what we are suppose to be" - Albert Hofmann

"Through my LSD experience and my new picture of reality. I became aware of the wonder of creation, the magnificence of nature and the animal and plant kingdom. I became very sensitive to what will happen to all this and all of us." - Albert Hofmann

Albert Hofmann & LSD

When considering all these different types of experiences, whether it is the near-death or psychotropic experience, the common denominator appears to be a shift in consciousness to alternative states of reality. Although most of the mainstream scientific community would not like to admit it, human consciousness appears to exist independent of the biological brain and functions of the physical body. It is as though the body and brain are just vehicles which allow our consciousness to experience this earthly physical reality from a unique, independent and detached perspective, and when the body expires our conscious point of attention shifts back to where it once came, an ocean of timeless and limitless consciousness.

"I don't believe that consciousness is generated by the brain. I believe that the brain is more of a receiver of consciousness."
- Graham Hancock

"You are not limited to this body, to this mind, or to this reality, you are a limitless ocean of Consciousness, imbued with infinite potential. You are existence itself." - Joseph P. Kauffman

Notes for chapter 8

1) Buddy T. What to know about Peyote use. Verywell mind, 2020. https://www.verywellmind.com/how-long-does-peyote-stay-in-your-system-80310

2) Amanita Muscaria. https://en.wikipedia.org/wiki/Amanita_muscaria

3) Brian Rose, ayahuasca experience, back from the dead. London Real TV. 2018. https://www.youtube.com/watch?v=vCnk5Ed4_YA

4) Joe Rogan interview with Graham Hancock. Joe Rogan | Ayahuasca is Amazonian Science w/Graham Hancock. 2018. Youtube. https://www.youtube.com/watch?v=_hhNEvOloaw

5) Albert Hofmann, Wikipedia. https://en.wikipedia.org/wiki/Albert_Hofmann

Conclusion

It is clear that throughout human history many cultures, societies and individuals had mastered the art of transcending the limited constraints of their earthly bodies to view and even interact with other versions or dimensions of reality. Whether it is down to evolution or the intended consequence of God's creation of man, our limited sensory perception only allows a measured and restricted experience within a modest amount of time. The inquisitive desire to look outside ourselves, into alternative layers of Divine consciousness has been with us since man first looked out towards the heavens and saw the scale of infinite potential offered even by his own limited view.

This earthly physical plane appears to be the middle ground between what many consider to be heaven and hell. At one extreme, a world of divine light and at the other an underworld, a godless place devoid of that which the light has to offer. These two extremities seem to collide in our material world, a battleground offering each individual the ability to experience almost limitless variations of both these extremes in order to improve their own conscious development; each deciding how far their free will wishes to take them in either direction. This is essentially a cosmic version of the Hegelian dialectic, with a thesis (Heaven), an antithesis (the underworld) and a synthesis (our conscious development through life's experience).

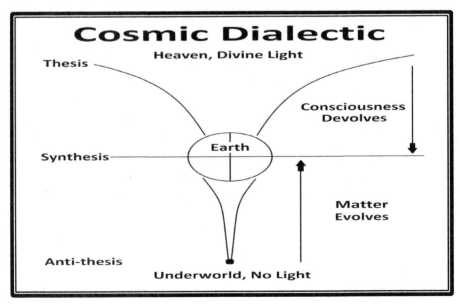

While aspects of Divine light devolve down into matter upon this earth, various expressions of anti-Divine energy are evolving upwards, manifesting in the form of malevolent entities eager to promote godless characteristics associated with the underworld, and over time will grow more sophisticated as they interact and oppose Divine consciousness here upon the earth.

In order for the overall development of consciousness to experience an almost unlimited amount of options, the Earth and the universe must be under some form of constant change; a mechanism of change which is variable enough to fulfil a variety of experiences but stable enough to allow the continuity of life. The zodiac clock of the great year, offering twelve ages or epochs, each 2160 years long, is a possible explanation and insight into how this balancing act of change can manifest, giving tremendous opportunity for varying cosmic energies to influence human consciousness over time.

At this present time, we find ourselves in the grip of global change not witnessed before on such an unprecedented scale. It could all be part of the grand design, the cosmic clock moving from the old Piscean epoch into the new Age of Aquarius. Saturn, the ruling planet of this new epoch, has the potential to promote and increase the activity and influence of entities and their representatives from the underworld, evolving upwards to impose satanic energies of controlling restrictions upon humanity for the next two epochs. The logic behind this observation comes from the characteristic expression of the planetary glyph associated with Saturn, which is the cross of materialism over the crescent of spirituality. This represents the order of priority where material matters take precedence over spiritual matters.

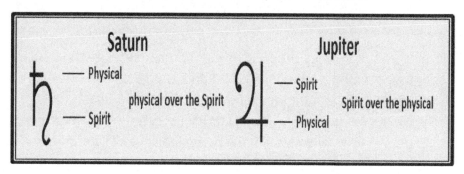

This new arrangement of cosmic influence, although subtle, could promote the ascension and involvement of some rather dark entities into our reality. Prior to this transition, Jupiter ruled the previous Age of Pisces, the Age of Belief where spiritual matters took precedence over material ones. It was an Age where spiritual energy and higher levels of consciousness devolved from the heavens to interact with our physical reality, it was a time of religious and spiritual expansion, when Jesus and Muhammad entered the picture promoting their unique expressions of spiritual matters. Now the opposite is the case, it is the 'Age of knowing', where the control system will be moving full steam ahead to impose its Satanic will over all of humanity.

This energetic change is subtle. However, if humanity, as a whole, sits back and does nothing to counteract Satanic energy, their lives will reflect this backdrop, but if they unite, in pockets of resistance, focusing on higher levels of spiritual consciousness, their righteous intent and will, as a collective, should tip the balance of light in their favour.

Added to this mix is the planet Uranus, occupying shared ruler-ship for the first one thousand years. This is the planet of new technology, revolution and independence. However, being an outer planet, not visible to the naked eye, its influence is primarily concerned with the subconscious. And although it will promote feelings of rebellion and independence the rulers of the material world will use new technology to dilute and restrict this energy from manifesting and disrupting the world which they are trying to create and control.

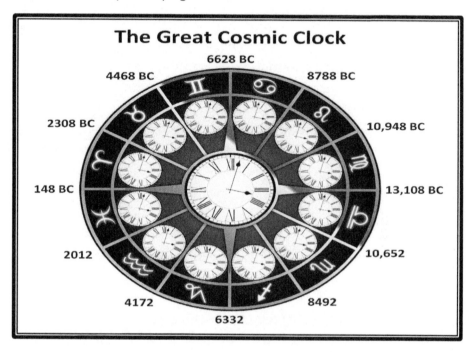

This new world created by Satanic forces is likely to be genetically modified and geo-engineered to restrict spiritual light while promoting dark and sinister objectives. The whole epoch will be a 180 degree paradigm shift focussing on material matters. The entities, which at the moment, largely inhabit lower worlds, may try to interface with humanity by transforming our natural biology towards a more artificially based humanoid, pulling us further away from nature's own balancing system. Pulling us away from the presence of divine light and limitless potential into a hellish world of automated and mechanised godlessness.

If this is all part of the divine cycle of ages, then we ultimately should have nothing to fear, as it is part of humanity's inevitable cycle to experience this reality from alternative profound perspectives. And as we reincarnate back into this realm, sometime in the future, to face new challenges, it should ultimately turn out as the Creator intended. Jupiter will once more rule the heavens 4300 years from now when we enter the Age of Sagittarius. This is essentially the second coming of Jupiter-Zues, when the optimistic and spiritual characteristics of this enormous planet will once again dominate the Age.

The Buddha tamed the Naga, Jesus and Muhammad suppressed sinister and satanic forces, setting a precedent for us to follow, showing us that it is possible to have dominion over the space humans occupy. However, during this new epoch it will be more difficult, than it was before, to free ourselves from the impositions of the control system. Therefore, it is up to us individually to decide how much of the light or darkness we allow into our lives. Furthermore, those who appreciate the concept of reincarnation should not fear the future as the cycle of life goes through inevitable changes which overall are part of the big plan. For this reason life should be lived and not taken as seriously as some would like to make it. Being aware of the immortality of the spirit helps us walk through life with an optimistic and jovial approach, where we can truly focus on the immediate moment as opposed to being regretful of the past or worried about the future. Living in the now is what we came here to experience, and only by doing this can we truly fulfil our karmic destiny, which will ultimately lead us back into higher states of consciousness.

Many people live in fear, for one reason or another. They fear death, they fear poverty, they fear illness. There are no limits to the array of potential fears offered, especially by those running the control system. In order to overcome these fears one must release this anxiety and realise that death is part of the living process and is something which we all came here to do. The result of this process takes our conscious attention out into other realities, liberating the awareness from any trauma associated with this present life. No matter in which realm you next find yourself, the light at the centre of creation is always there to pull you back if you only ask.

As we are all on unique individual paths of karmic development, to judge others by your own standards is pointless. The control system will try to pull the majority of people into underpinning and promoting their vision of the future as opposed to allowing those people to blossom under their own intuition and to live a life which gives them freedom and options. Mythology teaches us that if any control system oversteps its remit by uniting humanity under an all encompassing one size fits all arrangement Creator consciousness will intervene with its own divine reset, allowing the spectrum of diversity to manifest once more. This is exactly what happened in the Tower of babel narrative.

"A united humanity in the generations following the Great Flood, speaking a single language and migrating westward, comes to the land of Shinar. There they agree to build a city and a tower tall enough to reach heaven. God, observing their city and tower, confounds their speech so that they can no longer understand each other, and scatters them around the world." – Tower of Babel, Wikipedia

208

The Bible tells us that some form of barrier was placed between the Earth and Heaven in order to keep the sanctity and unique qualities of the higher realms from penetrating too much into the lower ones. This appears to corroborate the visions and sensations of those who have had near-death experiences, recollections of going through dark tunnels to emerge at the other end into a world of light.

"Then God said, "Let there be a firmament in the midst of the waters, and let it divide the waters from the waters." Thus God made the firmament, and divided the waters which were under the firmament from the waters which were above the firmament; and it was so. And God called the firmament Heaven. So the evening and the morning were the second day." - Genesis 1 : 6-8 (NKJV)

The universe appears to have its own built in mechanism for resetting the Earth through the unpredictable appearance of comets. No matter how advanced humanity becomes or how far entities from the underworld infest this earthly realm, cosmic forces, out of our control, can, at any time, smash their way through our atmosphere sending the Earth and all its inhabitants back to the Stone Age, keeping the natural cycle of rising and falling civilisations ongoing.

When a person no longer resonates with their own unique song, unable or unwilling to live a life according to one's own moral compass, instead conforming to the requirements of others, they are essentially sacrificing their own unique potential to fit in with a choir who's conductor has motives of his own. The vast majority of people avoid walking a path towards fulfilling their destiny, opting instead to sell their dreams for security, as social expectations pen them in from breaking free to discover who they really are and what they truly came here for. Life is a journey of risks and those who sit back frightened of taking any chances have already died inside. Within this earthly battleground, and the fight between light and dark forces, each one of us moves one step closer towards their own physical deaths. I would suggest that those people who choose to ignore their deep intuitive calling in life, prompting them into exploring their own unique qualities are not fully awake and are not truly living. They say only the good die young, maybe there is some truth in this. For the majority of people trapped throughout the world within the web of the control system, are, on average, living longer whilst being caught within the monotony of mundane repetition. With many not having yet fulfilled their purpose for coming here, their advancing years present the opportunity of more time to break free as they fade further into old age. Is it the case that whatever disposition, obsession or perversion you develop and attach to your thoughts, during the final stages of your life, will ultimately have an influence on the kind of reality you enter into after this one had expired?

When viewing the lives of our ancestors, much of what they created and strived for has faded, along with the memories of their cultures and civilisations. Consequently, one may ask, what was the true underlining purpose of their living experience if it was not to interact with one another in a manner favourable to their overall spiritual and conscious development?

With all this considered, it is still a beautiful world, and it is up to all of us to find our true place within it. Be yourself, strive to be happy and love one another.

"We are spirits descended into matter for a purpose. Understanding this is the meaning of the term having life, and having it more abundantly. This does not mean accumulation of products. It means doing that which is true. Truth is eternal. It cannot alter. Only truth will make you free." - Alan Watt, Cutting through, volume 1

Author's Bio

Brian Taylor was born in a small town in the suburbs of Nottingham, England during the late 1960s. After graduating with BSc (Hons) in construction management from Leeds Polytechnic in 1992, he spent most of his time working as an engineer. After many years fascinated by the bigger questions of life, he chose to take time away from western society, to pursue a journey of discovery. With an open mind and an optimistic belief in himself, he decided to see where destiny would take him.

During his many years travelling mostly throughout Southeast Asia, he discovered the answers to many of the questions which he had been carrying for years. At this time he wrote two books, the first one entitled *'Language of the Gods'*, was a comprehensive breakdown of how the controlling elite divide and rule humanity from a physical perspective, with an astrological overtone. His second book *'Metaphysics of the Gods'* looked into how universal energies are the building blocks for our perception of reality, within a feed-back loop of human consciousness. At this stage in his journey, he began to understand the mechanisms in play relating to how we influence our reality. A profound moment, and the most important and valuable lesson an individual can learn in a limited lifetime. From this core knowledge he revisited history to see if it made more sense. This was when he wrote *'Metaphysics of WW2'*.

As the years progressed Mr Taylor noticed an increase in obesity in western tourists visiting Southeast Asia. American and British tourists in particular, appeared to have developed some unhealthy eating habits in comparison to the Asians, who, on the whole, ate a relatively healthy and modest diet. This prompted Mr Taylor to investigate the subject from a metaphysical perspective, not only to benefit others, but also himself. This resulted in the book *'The Metaphysical Diet'*. To add to the series of books on metaphysics and suspecting that humanity was being steered in a direction which was not entirely righteous Mr Taylor next decided to investigate Kabbalah in relation to astrotheology and the globalisation project. This resulted in his book *'The Left Hand Path'*.

Finally, after more years of travelling and still evermore fascinated and puzzled by life's deeper questions, Mr Taylor focused on research regarding our connection to the spirit realm. This resulted in the book *'When The Spirit Takes Over'*.

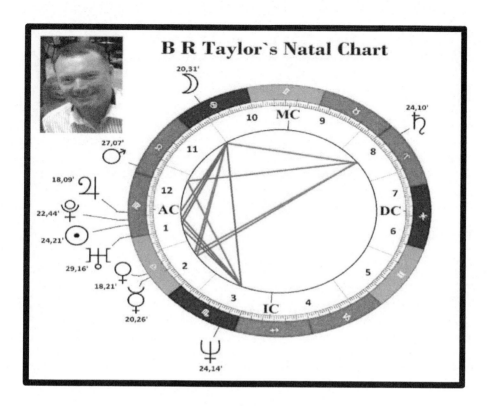

B R Taylor's Natal Chart

Other books by this author

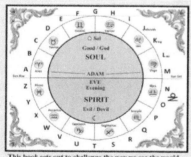

This book sets out to challenge the way we see the world, our adopted belief systems and coordinates within world history. It exposes how the potential of a united humanity has been suppressed by various forms of control over thousands of years, elites which have used division in both our physical and spiritual realms. The book is a journey of discovery into our true connection to the universe, and the relationship between the macrocosm and microcosm. The reader will come away with a fresh empowering view of how planetary cycles and energies along with human consciousness are the drivers behind geopolitical events and the ever changing fortunes of time.

"We are what we think. All that we are arises with our thoughts. With our thoughts, we make the world." Buddha

Language of the Gods

B R TAYLOR

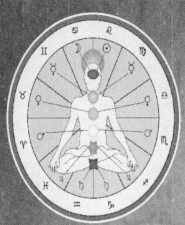

Metaphysics of the Gods

"And i saw in the right hand of him that sat on the throne a book written within and on the backside, sealed with seven seals."
Revelation 5:1

Metaphysics of the Gods

B R Taylor

B R Taylor

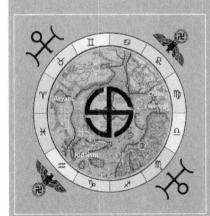

Metaphysics of WW2

If you think you understand WW2, think again! Until you have looked into the metaphysical (beyond the physical) aspect of the subject, together with the astrological timing in which it took place, you really are only scratching the surface. Many war historians and scholars concern themselves with the people, places and events surrounding WW2, but neglect the bigger picture. This is the only book of its kind to give you the big picture.

Metaphysics of WW2

B R Taylor

B R Taylor

The Metaphysical Diet

The Metaphysical Diet

B R Taylor

The Metaphysical Diet

Only recently has the three meal a day mentality become accepted as the norm. We are a generation overeating. Our habitual nature has been hijacked and steered in a sinister and unhealthy direction, in order to underpin and support a corporate system reliant on excessive consumption. Most diets fail because they focus on momentary solutions to deep rooted problems. This is the only book of its kind to explain the astrological and metaphysical mechanisms at play behind obesity, and how, without spending a fortune, one can learn to sow new seeds of health, wealth and happiness within the powerful mind of the subconscious.

B R Taylor

The Left Hand Path

The Left Hand Path

B R Taylor

The word sinister comes from the Latin for left. It is the new direction for humanity. This book examines Kabbalistic, astrological and occult forces behind the new globalisation project, exposing its sinister left hand agenda as we move further into the new Aquarian Age.

B R Taylor

Websites by this author

www.BRTaylorMetaphysics.com

B R Taylor's Youtube channel

https://www.youtube.com/channel/UC6Ic7_8H0JGdrDhpQWuvfBQ

https://www.bitchute.com/channel/O60Mhc33iUmU/

https://brandnewtube.com/@BRTaylor

https://odysee.com/@BRTaylorMataphysics:b

https://twitter.com/BRTaylor14

Printed in Great Britain
by Amazon

67853065R00129